LISTENERS' GUIDE TO MEDIEVAL ENGLISH

GARLAND REFERENCE LIBRARY
OF THE HUMANITIES
(VOL. 912)

LISTENERS' GUIDE TO MEDIEVAL ENGLISH
A Discography

Betsy Bowden

GARLAND PUBLISHING, INC. • NEW YORK & LONDON
1988

© 1988 by Betsy Bowden
All rights reserved

LIBRARY OF CONGRESS
Library of Congress Cataloging-in-Publication Data

Bowden, Betsy.
  Listeners' guide to medieval English : a discography / Betsy Bowden.
    p. cm. — (Garland reference library of the humanities ; vol. 912)
    Bibliography: p.
    Includes index.
    ISBN 0-8240-6347-3 (alk. paper)
    1. English language—Middle English, 1100–1500—Discography.
2. English language—Old English, ca. 450–1100—Discography.
3. Chaucer, Geoffrey, d. 1400—Discography. 4. Beowulf—Discography. 5. English language—Middle English, 1100–1500—Study and teaching—Audio-visual aids—Catalogs. 6. English language—Old English, ca. 450–1100—Study and teaching—Audio-visual aids—Catalogs. 7. English literature—Discography. I. Title.
II. Series.
Z5818.E5B68 1988
[PE519]
016.427'02—dc19   88-24325
                                                                     CIP

Printed on acid-free, 250-year-life paper
Manufactured in the United States of America

For Ken,
who did not prepare my index

CONTENTS

ARRANGED ACCORDING TO RECORD COMPANY AND STOCK NUMBER
(N.B.: See Index for listing according to works of literature.)

Abbreviations:
Besides the abbreviated titles of Chaucer's works, listed alphabetically in the Index, and besides *SGGK* for *Sir Gawain and the Green Knight*, throughout this discography ME means Middle English, ModE Modern English, and OE Old English. See Appendix for full names of record companies abbreviated.

Acknowledgments	xi
Introduction	xiii
Bibliography	xxvii
ANZAMRS. 1 (PF)	3
Argo. SAY 23 (WBP, WBT)	4
SAY 73 (ModE)	6
SAY 107 (Everyman)	7
PLP 1001, now SAY 24 (GP)	7

Argo, cont.
   PLP 1002, now SAY 91 (NPT, PLGW,
      Chaucerian short poems) 9
   ZPL 1003-4, now SAY 74 (Tr) 11
   ZPL 1008 (ME lyrics, Kingis Quair) 13
   ZPL 1208-10, now SAY 91 (KnT) 14
   ZPL 1211, now SAY 24 (PardT) 17
   (Z)RG (5)443 (ME lyrics) 20
Bellerophon. (GP) 20
Caedmon. TC/SWC 1008 (NPT, PardT) 22
   TC/SWC 1021 (PLGW) 23
   SWC 1030 (ME banns) 25
   SWC 1031 (Everyman) 25
   SWC 1032 (ModE) 25
   SWC 1054 (Malory) 26
   TC/SWC 1102 (ModE) 26
   TC/SWC 1130 (ModE) 26
   TC/CDL5 1151 (GP, ParsP, Retraction) 27
   SWC 1161 (Beowulf, various OE works) 28
   TC/SWC 1192 (SGGK, Pearl) 29
   SWC 1223 (M1rT, RvT) 29
   TC/SWC 1226 (PF, Chaucerian short poems) 31
   SWC 1374 (Malory) 33
   SWC 1424 (various OE works) 33
   SWC/CDL5/TC 3008 (GP, Astr, various OE and
      ME works) 33
   TC/CDL5 4001 (Beowulf) 35
Cambridge. (Chaucer not reviewed) 35
Capitol. SW 229 (ModE) 36
Cassette Book Company. 853 (ModE) 36
Columbia. AMS 6198 (GP, WBP) 37
Decca. DL 9418 (ME lyrics) 38
Deutsche Grammophon. 139380 (ModE) 38
EAV. KE 0296, formerly LE 7733B (WBP, WBT) 39
   LE 7650-55 (GP, Tr, various OE and ME works) 41

Contents

EAV, cont.
KE 90233B (GP, NPT)	43
KE 90395, formerly LE 5055 (GP, WBP, PriT, Tr, Beowulf)	45
English Classics. XTV 17216-17 (NPT)	47
Everest. 3145/7, formerly Esoteric ES 521 (ME lyrics)	49
Everett/Edwards. (Chaucer not reviewed)	49
Experiences Anonymes. EA 0024, later MHS 678 (ME lyrics)	50
EA 0029 (ME lyrics)	50
Folkways. SC 9851 (WBT, SGGK, various OE works)	51
FL 9858 (various OE works)	52
FL 9859 (GP, PardT, NPT, Chaucerian short poems)	53
Golden Clarioun. 1RR (Rom)	55
2BD (BD)	56
3HF(1), 3HF(2) (HF)	57
5PF (PF)	59
6Tr(1), 6Tr(2) (Tr)	61
10GP (GP)	65
10GPB (GP)	66
11KnT (KnT)	68
12MiT (M1rT)	70
13ReT (RvT)	71
16WBP (WBP)	72
16WBT (WBT)	73
17FrT (FriT)	75
18SuT (SumT)	76
19ClT (ClT)	78
20MeT (MctT)	79
22FkT (FrkT)	81
24PdT (PardT)	82

Golden Clarioun, cont.
   26PrT, 27TST (PriT, Thop)   84
   30NPT (NPT)   87
   40Ga(1), 40Ga(2), 40Ga(3) (SGGK)   88
   41Pl (Pearl)   89
   44SrO (Sir Orfeo)   89
   45Ly (ME lyrics)   89
   46Pi (Piers Plowman)   90
   70No (Towneley Noah)   91
Harmonia Mundi. HM 1106 (ME lyrics)   91
Hyperion. A66094 (ME lyrics)   92
Linguaphone. (GP, PriT)   92
Listen for Pleasure. 7101 (ModE)   93
Medieval Sounds. M-1 (GP, PardT)   93
MHS. 4485 (ME lyrics)   95
NCTE. EMC-65-2963/4 (NPT, Beowulf)   96
   45787, formerly RL20-8 (various Chaucerian works)   97
   P4PM-4852 (GP, NPT, Beowulf)   99
Nonesuch. H 71315 (PriT, OE and ME passages)   100
Oelsen Films. 30/50 (ModE)   101
Plant Life. PLR 043 (ME lyrics)   101
Pleiades. P250 (ME lyrics)   102
Radio Arts. (Beowulf)   103
RCA. LM 6015 (ME lyrics)   103
Recording for the Blind. (Chaucer not reviewed)   104
Scott Foresman. P4RP-6532 (GP)   104
Spoken Arts. SA 918, SAC 7/8004 (Beowulf)   106
   SA 919, SAC 7/8004 (GP, PardT)   106
Spoken Word. 1 (GP)   108
   99705-11 (ModE)   109
   99712-X (Everyman)   112
Appendix: Record Company Addresses   113

Index
- I. Chaucer Recordings, Arranged According to Abbreviated Titles of Works, with Readers or Performers — 119
- II. Recordings of Middle English Excluding Chaucer, Arranged According to Known Author or Common Title, with Readers or Performers — 124
- III. Recordings of Old English, Arranged According to Known Author or Common Title, with Readers — 126

ACKNOWLEDGMENTS

This discography had its origins within the pamphlet series produced by TEAMS, the interdisciplinary pedagogical organization associated with the Medieval Institute at Kalamazoo, Michigan. Sue Ellen Holbrook provided the idea and initial impetus; she nursed this work through two drafts, complete with outside readers' comments, before it outgrew TEAMS's format and resources. Other essential assistance came from Susan Crane, who read an early draft and all along provided help with pronunciation issues as well as encouragement concerning life in general. For general encouragement I likewise thank Tom Burton, Charles Muscatine, Alan Gaylord, Howell D. Chickering, Jr., and my parents, Edward and Ruth Bowden. Several record companies generously supplied review copies: ANZAMRS, Argo, Caedmon, Cassette Book Company, EAV, Folkways, Golden Clarioun, Medieval Sounds, and NCTE. Among the many librarians and media-room attendants who assisted, I especially appreciate extra efforts by those at Rutgers University in Camden, the University of Pennsylvania, the Free Library of Philadelphia, and the University of New Hampshire.

Thomas C. Moser, Jr., and Burton Raffel both sent information that I requested while they were in the process of moving; Jeanne Lance and Andrew Mirer intervened with the New York Public Library system; and Ida Levin and Rita Lorang typed the manuscript. The Research Council of Rutgers University provided financial assistance.

INTRODUCTION

In late-nineteenth-century universities, as curricula in Modern Languages began to replace Greek and Latin, pedagogical authorities decided that Shakespeare's language ought to be pronounced in each professor's own dialect, rather than that of Elizabethan London, whereas one should attempt to pronounce Chaucer's language as he himself did. The earliest teachers of Chaucer, such as Francis James Child and George Lyman Kittredge, punctuated their lectures with dramatic readings of the Middle English text in laboriously reconstructed pronunciation.

Nowadays most Chaucer professors continue this pedagogical practice, using their voices to lift from the page the oddly spelled words and shape them into full-color characters for their students. Many medievalists do not perform, however, silenced by the same qualms that may constrain their nonmedievalist colleagues who teach Chaucer units in survey courses—by apprehension that their stumbling on Middle English pronunciation might ruin, rather than enhance, students' understanding.

Fortunately, technology has kept pace with the rapid expansion of English as an academic field. During the past four decades, dozens of medievalists and other performers have recorded early English. Many educational institutions already own one or more sound recordings of English before 1500, or may wish to purchase the most useful ones available. This discography is meant to help teachers, administrators, and librarians make the best use of their resources.

Professionals need to know exactly what passages a recording contains, especially one with an inexplicit title such as *Canterbury Tales* or *Medieval Poetry*. They need to know that those passages are read in the original language, since cover information is sometimes so imprecise that a recording reveals itself as a Modern English translation only when played. Certainly, too, they might want to know whether a given performance is worth hearing: most readers on educational media pronounce Middle English correctly, but not all can act. A poor performance could irreparably convince students that Chaucer belongs in a dreary monotone.

What makes a bad performance bad? As discussed below under "11. Evaluation," the issue has seldom been raised, never before for Chaucer. The evaluations in this discography constitute the first published set of aesthetic judgments on oral performances of Chaucer's text. It has not seemed useful to evaluate recordings of Old English or Middle English other than Chaucer's, however. Nonmedievalists seldom teach these works in the original. Medievalists disagree on pronunciation and meter of dialects other than Chaucer's. In nearly every case, besides, they can estimate the probable value of the acting by checking performances of Chaucer by the same reader.

Why pass aesthetic judgments at all, though, on readings-aloud of Chaucer's works? The implications go beyond pragmatic pedagogy. Much twentieth-century

Introduction

Chaucer criticism has centered on issues first raised by Kittredge, who carefully described character's voices in the pilgrimage drama that he envisioned. For example, the Pardoner tells the other pilgrims how he cheats gullible churchgoers. After his exemplary tale he invokes Christ's pardon in—according to Kittredge—"a very paroxysm of agonized sincerity," and then tries to sell pardons to the pilgrims in "a wild orgy of reckless jesting" (217). Reams have since been written on the Pardoner's exact tone of voice in *PardT* 916-18: hushed sincerity, fake sincerity, flagrant insincerity, formulaic benediction, and so on. Extended critical arguments have likewise centered on the Merchant's tone of voice describing his shrewish wife (bitter? resigned? joking?), on the Nun's Priest's tone of voice at the close of his tale (didactic? ironic? amused?), and certainly on the voices within voices of the General Prologue, spoken by a naive Chaucer-the-pilgrim who has been created by Chaucer-the-author to express (perhaps) the ideas of Chaucer-the-man.

Because evaluations in this discography center on these and other much-discussed passages, nonmedievalists will find here a convenient review of twentieth-century Chaucer scholarship directly applicable to specific classroom situations. Medievalists in other disciplines, such as art history, will find the same. Chaucerians themselves, including those who regularly perform and even record for their own students, will find in addition a feast worthy of the Franklin, of food for thought.

Suppose that a Chaucer scholar has always, both silently and out loud, read the Wife of Bath's attitude toward encroaching old age as one of hearty self-sufficiency (*WBP* 469-79). This professor can discover that, in one enactment, the Wife instead shrugs aside old age as a minor annoyance, whereas in an equally well-performed one she speaks the same lines with sighs and bitter resentment (Argo SAY 23, Golden Clarioun 16WBP). The scholar can seek out the recordings, listen, and think through the import of such dissimilar dramatizations, both for the classroom and for literary analysis of this text that Chaucer wrote with oral delivery in mind. Throughout six centuries, Chaucer's words have come to life in readers' minds—regarded always as great literature, always for different reasons. By seeking and analyzing those textual characteristics that create the potential for flexibility in performance and in imagined performance, critics can come to consider what makes some literature last through the centuries and thereby what makes great literature great.

Although teachers and theoreticians for some 25 centuries have been considering what makes great literature great, it was not until approximately 110 years after the introduction of printing that the Stationers' Company began to keep track of books published in London. Today, 110 years after the invention of sound recording, the need for a Stationers' Register is acute but unfilled. The commercial recording industry, if it can even be termed an entity, has nothing resembling a permanent reference source. (See introduction to Appendix: Record Company Addresses.) The companies that make and sell educational recordings sometimes retain no information on their own items no longer produced. (See note on Cambridge UP recordings.) Ordinary bibliographic methods are ineffectual at best and misleading at worst, since no standard cataloguing form has been adopted for sound recordings. (See below under "2. Title.") By far the best information-gathering technique is serendipity.

Accordingly, this discography has been compiled by going to scores of places in Philadelphia, Washington, Boston, New York City, New Jersey, New Hampshire,

Introduction xvii

New Mexico, California, and everywhere else the author visited in the course of several years, and there checking card catalogues and unsorted record bins in public and university libraries, music listening rooms, language labs, audiovisual rooms, and English Department closets. Collections are unpredictable. Slippery Rock University owns over a dozen Chaucer recordings, including several found nowhere else; Harvard owns just two.

Probably this discography includes nearly all Chaucer recordings ever distributed commercially. It is less likely to be complete for other Old and Middle English. Even serendipity falters without an exact album title, when one cannot check under "C" for Chaucer. For example, this discography includes only the Towneley *Noah* play in Middle English (Golden Clarioun 70No); all other cycle plays are in ModE translation. Has somebody somewhere, presumably with a small record company, usefully recorded other drama in Middle English, for the benefit of students who could thereby understand and indeed perform a frequently anthologized play like the *Secunda Pastorum*?

Because the author has personally looked at and listened to every Chaucer recording in this discography, information concerning them is fuller than for recordings that contain only Old and Middle English other than Chaucer's. For example, sometimes a record company is unable to supply the exact lines excerpted from *Beowulf*.

More reference materials exist for music than for spoken-word recordings. Therefore, this discography accounts for several albums that consist exclusively of Middle English lyric songs (sometimes read as poems), plus a sampling from the numerous albums of international medieval music that include one or two ME songs. (See Couver/Colvig and Croucher for song-by-song listings. Only "Sumer is icumen in " is indexed separately here.)

Information concerning each recording is organized into ten categories, plus an eleventh (Evaluation) for those that include Chaucer. Despite complications noted below, the two most stable features by which to distinguish one recording from another, similarly titled one are record company name and stock number. This discography is arranged alphabetically by the former, then numerically by the latter. For each recording the following information appears, line by line:

1. Record company name, stock number, medium, availability.

a) Record company name. (See the Appendix for full names of those abbreviated.) Some companies have changed their names, and some distribute each other's recordings; such complications are noted if discovered.

b) Stock number. In the accelerating shift from records to cassette tapes, some record companies have kept stock number constant. Caedmon TC 1008 and SWC 1008 refer to the same performance, for example, the former on a record and the latter on tape. Other companies, as noted both in each entry and in the Table of Contents, have changed stock number along with medium.

c) Medium. An item may be a record or a cassette tape, with indication here too of former states and of several-unit sets. Each Chaucer performance is evaluated as it sounds in the medium actually listened to. In reference to a record, even for a performance now produced only on cassette, full details of cover and enclosures are also given. The many advantages of cassette tapes do not include reliable sound quality or space for printed information. Records frequently include a copy of the exact text being read, for example, whereas cassettes seldom do.

d) Availability. Only unavailability is noted. Thus, a blank here means that, in 1985-87, the performance was still

Introduction xix

for sale in the medium described. Recordings no longer produced may, of course, still be found in libraries and elsewhere.

2. Title. Different recordings from different companies can have the same title. Identification by title is further complicated in that no system is agreed upon by record companies or librarians, much less by (say) work-study students filing tapes in a language lab. Thus, for example, the same recording might well appear entitled *The Canterbury Tales, by Chaucer / The Prologue*, or *Prologue of Canterbury Tales (Chaucer)*, or *Chaucer, Geoffrey / General Prologue to the Canterbury Tales*, or any number of variations, depending on somebody's familiarity with Chaucer and/or sense as to what appears most important on the record cover.

3. Reader(s) of Old and Middle English, if given (or performers of music).

4. Date of production, if given.

5. Other production information, if given, such as series title, director, producer, sponsor, and reader(s) of ModE translations.

6. Identification number(s) other than stock number, if given.

7. Edition being read aloud. For works other than Chaucer's, citations are only as complete as record companies were able to provide. For Chaucer, full bibliographic information is supplied *only if* the reading certainly comes from an edition *other than* the one that has long remained standard: F. N. Robinson, ed., *The Works of Geoffrey Chaucer*, 2d ed. (Boston: Houghton Mifflin, 1957), published in Britain by Oxford UP. Assume Robinson unless told otherwise, that is.

If the record company both uses and credits Robinson's second edition, the credit is mentioned under "Cover" or

"Enclosure(s)" as appropriate (see 9 and 10 below). Surprisingly often, though, no attribution appears for a text read or even reproduced. In several cases I have determined the edition by correspondence with the record company or the reader. In the remaining cases, I have determined by ear that a student could follow the reading while looking at Robinson's second edition.

8. Contents and location. Passages are listed as they occur on each side of the recording, in order, and on each band for records so divided. Also noted are duration times of sides or of selections, if given, and press numbers, if given. Information is less complete for the recordings of works other than Chaucer's, since not all were examined.

All Chaucer references are to line numbers in Robinson's second edition, even if the record cover or enclosure numbers lines differently. Texts with records, like texts in literature anthologies, often begin numbering a Canterbury tale at line one, rather than as a part of its fragment. Users of this discography can align such instances with Robinson's readily available second edition.

9. Cover. I report what was actually present on the record cover or cassette label examined. In several cases, librarians had taped a record or had replaced a commercial cover with a sturdier, blank one.

10. Enclosure(s). I report what was actually enclosed with the item examined. In several cases, materials might have been removed by library patrons. Availability (only) of multiple copies of an enclosure is noted here.

11. Evaluation. This category is omitted for recordings that contain no Chaucerian material and for ModE translations. For mixed recordings, only the Chaucer portion is evaluated. Judgments on Chaucer performances cover three elements: pronunciation, pedagogical practicality, and performance.

Introduction xxi

a) Pronunciation. A century of philological research has resulted in a generally accepted reconstruction of nearly all the sounds of Middle English. This discography makes no attempt to chart readers' choices on the few vowels still under contention, such as short *a* and diphthong *ay/ey*. Instead, for practical reasons, it notes agreed-on deviations from the phonetic values most widely regarded as standard, those prescribed by Helge Kökeritz. (See EAV 90395.)

Besides sheer number of deviations from this norm of Kökeritz, including some on the recordings he himself made, another criterion for judgment is consistency. A ME word always mispronounced as its ModE cognate disrupts the performance less than does switching back and forth between two pronunciations, usually of a shifted vowel.

b) Pedagogical practicality. How has it been determined that students will come to understand Middle English more effectively from a recording in which a vowel is consistently modernized than from one in which the reader alternates ME and ModE? It has not. Perhaps someday educational theorists will determine what works best in this and other aural situations. In the meantime, "pedagogical practicality" here refers to the mechanics of using a given recording in a classroom or language lab.

Some mechanics are obvious. A cassette is easier to carry to class than a record, and can be wound in advance to play one excerpt. A record with band divisions is versatile, for playing several excerpts. A record without band divisions is far less adaptable, unless a class plan happens to coincide with passages that begin each side of the record. In language labs or at home, of course, it is possible to tape the desired portions of a record.

On the other hand, a record has better sound quality than a cassette, until scratched. Nothing very unexpected can happen to a record, furthermore, whereas tape players have been known to chew up or tangle or erase tapes in the best-planned classes. For minor problems, remember that most students in the room know more about cassette players than you do, and that at least one will be an expert.

Besides medium, gaps in the text being read affect pedagogical usefulness. To understand Middle English aurally, students must follow the words visually. If the reading skips without warning, the teacher must either spend class time having students mark passages, or else provide separate texts of the exact lines read. On-tape announcements of lines being skipped are even more essential for students expected to listen alone in language labs, yet only Golden Clarioun consistently provides this format.

One other consideration applies to readings meant to teach Middle English as a language. To learn to pronounce, students must repeat each sound just heard. The otherwise problematic NCTE 45787 provides this format. In contrast, on several recordings a scholar simply reads aloud a list of ME sounds and ModE words as examples, briskly, thus blocking aural absorption of the information.

c) Performance. The bulk of each evaluation concerns performance. Performance analysis was conceived along with sound recording and finally born in the 1970s, attended by an assortment of folklorists, anthropologists, rhetoricians, musicologists, actors, and linguists. It is still in its infancy, its methodology in flux. Yet it traces its ancestry to the earliest literary commentary, for Plato and Aristotle were raising issues about literature as performed, not as read silently. In England before 1500, also, historical evidence shows that silent reading seemed an eccentric aberration.

Literary scholars so far have not dealt head-on with the impact of performance analysis on literary aesthetics, in part because universities tend to discourage interdisciplinary research but in largest part, probably, simply because recording technology itself keeps changing at an astounding rate. In my own two books, studies of literature as performed by Bob Dylan and by Chaucer scholars respectively, I firmly refrain from aesthetic judgment during close comparisons of different oral performances of the same text.

Analysts in performance-oriented disciplines likewise avoid aesthetic issues. A few linguists, using machines, are investigating how the human voice conveys recognizable emotions. A few scholars of oral interpretation have tried to systematize listeners' responses to good and bad readings-aloud by adapting musicological terms for such features as pauses, pitch shifts, and tempo. Folklorists and anthropologists supply a strong commitment to performance analysis, having long regretted the meager appearance of oral texts on the page as compared with their full and subtly conveyed meanings in performance context. While experimenting with a wide range of analytic techniques, they agree that aesthetic judgment is a particularly complex issue not amenable to intercultural simplification. On a track parallel to these practical developers of performance analysis, meanwhile, run literary theorists who question the validity of aesthetic judgment passed on a text by any one reader at any one time. (See Bibliography for works related to performance analysis from these various perspectives.)

Because scholars from such a wide range of performance-related disciplines are currently raising so many theoretical and practical considerations, it would be injudicious to claim universal applicability for the aesthetic criteria being first developed in this discography. These specific criteria do apply to texts written by Geoffrey Chaucer in the fourteenth century and performed by twentieth-century readers whose native language is Modern

English. Each evaluative essay, besides treating pronunciation and pedagogical practicality, addresses the following questions concerning the aesthetics of performing Chaucer.

—Do personal attitudes of the reader interfere with a listener's comprehension of the text? For example, does a reader sound bored or pompous or angry or sleepy when no character in the text is expressing boredom or pomposity or anger or somnolence?

—Do the characters in the text, including the narrator, respond audibly to each others' expressed emotions, actions, and attitudes?

—Is each character consistently portrayed, especially when one reappears in the story after intervening material?

—Does the reader use vocal variety to convey textual action or description during monologues and the narrator's parts?

—Does the reader convey complexity that approximates, or even surpasses, that which silent readers have articulated for publication? A skillful performer, instead of resolving or simplifying textual ambiguity, is able to make it audible. Thus a listener can wonder about Criseyde's motivations, for example, as creatively as could a silent reader.

—Does the performance perhaps present new, potentially valid ways of interpreting that complex text? Or, if the performance communicates an agreed-on interpretation, does it do so clearly and articulately? For example, could someone come to understand the useful distinction between Chaucer-the-pilgrim and Chaucer-the-author by hearing a given performance of the General Prologue?

In this discography the evaluative essays have not been organized as lists of answers to all these questions. If mispronunciation or other problems loom so large that I

Introduction

recommend against a given recording, I do not go into detail about bad acting besides. Essays remain brief, likewise, for short passages out of narrative context (e.g., for those meant to demonstrate the history of the English language).

Many correctly pronounced recordings do intend dramatization, however. For each of these I provide evidence, citing line numbers, that exemplifies aesthetic pros and cons in enough detail that a Chaucerian or a nonspecialist teacher of Chaucer or a librarian can make an informed choice among several different performances of the same work. I hope thereby that this discography will help professionals create future generations of enthusiastic readers and teachers of the Father of English Literature, by using his intended mode of delivery.

BIBLIOGRAPHY

Alcheringa/Ethnopoetics. Journal on oral poetics, 1970-80.
Bacon, Wallace A. "An Aesthetics of Performance." *Literature in Performance* 1 (1980): 1-9.
Bäuml, Franz H. "Varieties and Consequences of Medieval Literacy and Illiteracy." *Speculum* 55 (1980): 237-65.
Beardsley, Monroe C. "Right Readings and Good Readings." *Literature in Performance* 1 (1980): 10-22.
Bowden, Betsy. *Performed Literature: Words and Music by Bob Dylan.* Bloomington: Indiana UP, 1982.
———. *Chaucer Aloud: The Varieties of Textual Interpretation.* Philadelphia: U of Pennsylvania P, 1987.
Clanchy, M. T. *From Memory to Written Record: England, 1066-1307.* Cambridge: Harvard UP, 1979.
Couver, James, and Richard Colvig. *Medieval and Renaissance Music on Long-Playing Records: Supplement, 1962-1971.* Detroit Studies in Music Bibliography 26. Detroit: Information Coordinators, 1973.
Crosby, Ruth C. "Oral Delivery in the Middle Ages." *Speculum* 11 (1936): 88-110.

———. "Chaucer and the Custom of Oral Delivery." *Speculum* 13 (1938): 413-32.
Croucher, Trevor, comp. *Early Music Discography, from Plainsong to the Sons of Bach.* 2 vols. Phoenix: Oryx Press, 1981.
Crystal, David. *The English Tone of Voice: Essays in Intonation, Prosody and Paralanguage.* New York: St. Martin's, 1976.
Duggan, Joseph J., ed. *Oral Literature: Seven Essays.* New York: Barnes & Noble, 1975.
Dundes, Alan. "Texture, Text, and Context." *Southern Folklore Quarterly* 28 (1964): 251-65.
Fine, Elizabeth. *The Folklore Text: From Performance to Print.* Bloomington: Indiana UP, 1984.
Finnegan, Ruth. *Oral Poetry: Its Nature, Significance and Social Context.* Cambridge: Cambridge UP, 1977.
Forrest, William Craig. "Literature as Aesthetic Object: The Kinesthetic Stratum." *Journal of Aesthetics and Art Criticism* 27 (1969): 455-59.
Georges, Robert A. "Toward an Understanding of Storytelling Events." *Journal of American Folklore* 82 (1969): 313-28.
Havelock, Eric. *Preface to Plato.* Cambridge: Harvard UP, 1963.
Holub, Robert C. *Reception Theory: A Critical Introduction.* New York: Methuen, 1984.
Jauss, Hans Robert. "The Alterity and Modernity of Medieval Literature." *New Literary History* 10 (1979): 181-229.
Kittredge, George Lyman. *Chaucer and His Poetry.* Cambridge: Harvard UP, 1915.
Kökeritz, Helge. *A Guide to Chaucer's Pronunciation.* 1961. Rpt. Toronto: U of Toronto P, in association with the Mediaeval Academy of America, 1978.

Lindahl, Carl. *Earnest Games: Folkloric Patterns in the Canterbury Tales.* Bloomington: Indiana UP, 1987.

Literature in Performance. Journal on oral interpretation, 1980- .

Loesch, Katharine T. "Literary Ambiguity and Oral Performance." *Quarterly Journal of Speech* 51 (1965): 258-67.

New Literary History 8 (1977): 335-535. Issue on oral poetry.

New Literary History 16 (1984): 1-206. Issue on oral and written traditions in the Middle Ages.

Ong, Walter J. *Orality and Literacy: The Technologizing of the Word.* New York: Methuen, 1982.

Oral Tradition. Journal on oral literature, 1986- .

Rosenberg, Bruce. *The Art of the American Folk Preacher.* Oxford: Oxford UP, 1970.

Stock, Brian, *The Implications of Literacy: Written Language and Modes of Interpretation in the Eleventh and Twelfth Centuries.* Princeton: Princeton UP, 1983.

Toelken, Barre. *The Dynamics of Folklore.* Boston: Houghton Mifflin, 1979.

Tompkins, Jane P., ed. *Reader-Response Criticism, from Formalism to Post-Structuralism.* Baltimore: Johns Hopkins UP, 1980.

THE RECORDINGS

ANZAMRS, 1, cassette.
The Parlement of Foules.
Readers Francis de Vries, Kevin Magarey, John Gray, Michael Wright, Margaret Singer, Greg Waite, Tom Burton, Gary Simes, Stephanie Hollis, Rosemary Greentree, Andrew Lynch, Forrest Scott, Mary Dove. 1986.
Director T. L. Burton. Produced by The Chaucer Studio, in association with the Australian and New Zealand Association for Medieval and Renaissance Studies.
Side 1, *PF* 1-699.
Side 2, Blank.
Cover: Personnel.

Dame Nature lets slip one ModE cognate, and the turtledove two ("my" 620, "be" 510, "I" 587). Otherwise, all thirteen Chaucerians attain nearly flawless prounciation as they enact their separate roles and also recite in unison the birds' joint protests and closing song (*PF* 492-97, 680-92). Some choral variety is created by changing the voice combinations: females protest in *PF* 494-95, for example, and males in 496-97.

Variety thus created tends to distract from the text rather than interpret it, however. Similarly, the two liveliest-sounding characters seem more distracting than compelling when each bursts upon the calmly read scene. A jolly,

Pandarus-like Africanus chuckles heartily while shoving the dreamer through the gate at *PF* 155-68, and the second tercel—the plain-spoken one—with *PF* 450 roars out a warning that leads to harsh threats.

Elsewhere, attempted characterization can be detected. The third tercel becomes a J. Alfred Prufrock figure, switching at *PF* 478 from self-doubt to complete hopelessness concerning his chances with women. The goose hisses "Pessss" in a gooselike manner (*PF* 563). The duck sounds just like an indignant Donald, especially at *PF* 594-95; the merlin, with no such obvious aural ancestor, echoes that indignation while condemning the cuckoo in *PF* 610-16. The formel eagle inexplicably flirts with Nature, who replies in her usual slow stolid tone of carefully pronounced separate syllables (*PF* 639-65). The narrator speaks smoothly throughout, but displays little variation. He seems oblivious to the unclothed states of Beaute and Venus, for example, and he simply lists bird names without drawing aural attention to their characteristics (*PF* 225, 269-73, 330-64).

Although not monotonous overall, this performance nonetheless fails to fulfill the text's potential for dramatization. Its near-perfect pronunciation makes it suitable for many student uses, however.

ARGO, SAY 23, two-cassette set.
The Wife of Bath's Tale by Geoffrey Chaucer.
Readers Prunella Scales, Richard Bebb.
1978, 1982.
Director Derek Brewer, producer Peter Orr. In association with The British Council.
Side 1, *WBP* 1-322.
Side 2, *WBP* 323-626.

Side 3, *WBP* 627-856, WBT 857-951.
Side 4, *WBT* 952-1264.
Cover: Ellesmere ms. Wife of Bath. Paragraph implying that the tape contains only the *Wife of Bath's Tale* (i.e., not the Prologue as well).

This skillful interpretation of the ever-controversial Wife of Bath retains in performance some of the ambiguity of the written word. Initially shrill in her eagerness to seize center stage, she begins to draw the other pilgrims into her confidence. For example, in *WBP* 7 she shares the problem of multiple marriages, rather than fretting about it or denying its validity. She stands firm in all situations. Not evading scriptural precepts, she states what the text does say, especially concerning virginity (*WBP* 62-76). Just as firmly, rather than uttering a prayer or an idle curse with lines 525 and 530, she commands God to bless the souls of her fifth husband and of her friend.

In contrast, at *WBP* 826-27 the Argo Wife employs a hushed, prayerful tone to hope that God will bless Jankyn's soul now in His hands. Thus one textual ambiguity is orally resolved: her fifth husband has died recently. Her marital status is audible also in the delight with which she terms widows wise, at line 1027.

The Wife has been widowed before, of course. In her recreated monologue toward her first three husbands, she waxes indignant at each proverbial idea. She resents their attitudes no more than she resents the onset of "age," however, her tone on that word in line 474 echoing her tones of address toward them in *WBP* 235-378. Women must endure minor annoyances in life, among them old age and old husbands.

A male voice performs the Pardoner's comments at *WBP* 164-68 and 184-87, all three pilgrims in *WBP* 829-56, and the knight who seeks to learn what women most desire. The knight sounds dignified, elitist, and self-confident throughout, even in his plea at *WBT* 1058-61. At lines 1067 and 1098-1103 his direct insults encompass no sensitivity toward feelings of the aged, lower-class hag. She responds with dignity surpassing his, however, calmly teaching him precisely the manners he needs. Delight creeps into her pedagogical tone as she approaches transformation, followed by coquetry as she poses the "yong and fair" option in lines 1223-26. Thereupon her voice clearly switches from that of an old woman imitating a flirtatious young woman to that of a flirtatious and triumphant young woman.

Here and throughout Prologue and Tale, in short, a unified character speaks her mind to the pilgrims, quotes herself pretending to speak her mind to her old husbands, tells a story of a woman in control who pretends to speak her mind to her new husband, and so on. Such voices within voices are possible to imagine, but very difficult to project orally. Success in execution outweighs any disadvantages of occasional slips in pronunciation, such as an Anglicized first syllable on "used," and two "noght"s lacking *ghs* (lines 562, 19, 159).

ARGO, SAY 73, cassette.
Beowulf, The Battle of Maldon, and Other Old English
  Poems.
Frank Duncan, Prunella Scales, and others, reading Modern
  English from Kevin Crossley-Holland's translations.

Not in Old English.

ARGO, SAY 107, cassette.
The Moral Play of Everyman / Visions from Piers Plowman by William Langland.
Readers Cyril Luckham, Gerald Harper, Gary Watson.
1975.
Producer Peter Orr. ModE readers Richard Pasco, Frank Duncan, and others.
Edition: A.C. Cawley, ed., *Everyman* (Everyman's Library, 1956; Manchester UP, 1961).
Entire play. Excerpts from *Piers Plowman* in Nevill Coghill's ModE translation.

ARGO, PLP 1001, record. Now available only as part of a two-cassette set (with *PardT*), SAY 24.
Chaucer. The Canterbury Tales. The Prologue.
Readers Nevill Coghill, Norman Davis, John Burrow.
1965 (cassette 1982).
The English Poets from Chaucer to Yeats, recorded in association with The British Council and Oxford University Press. Director George Rylands.
Side 1 (ARG 2589), band 1, *GP* 1-117.
    band 2, *GP* 118-207.
    band 3, *GP* 208-308.
    band 4, *GP* 309-387.
    band 5, *GP* 388-444.
Side 2 (ARG 2590), band 1, *GP* 445-541.
    band 2, *GP* 542-622.
    band 3, *GP* 623-714.
    band 4, *GP* 715-858.
Cover: Brief biography of Chaucer. Excerpts from commentary on Chaucer by Hoccleve, Spenser,

Dryden, Blake. "The Language of Chaucer" by Norman Davis.

Enclosure (with the record): Eight-page booklet with entire text read, plus glosses. No credit given for edition or glosses.

This recording contains no pronunciation errors, just slight leanings of occasional vowels toward ModE. Its fully adequate dramatization is more appropriate in excerpts than full-length. The three readers, who take turns at one or two portraits apiece, do not convey a consistent attitude by a Chaucer/pilgrim figure. In some cases a narrator describes what he sees—an untroubled Parson doing his duty, for example. In other cases the reader imitates the attitude of the pilgrim. The Friar, Monk, and Merchant all eagerly justify their own activities, and the Shipman conveys to landlubbers the importance of his knowledge.

All readers do project a consistent form of covert disapproval toward certain questionable pilgrims. With studied casualness, pretending that sins do not matter while knowing full well that they do, narrators tell of the Physician's love for gold, the Wife's love for the old dance, the Franklin's overspending on luxury foods, and the Pardoner's usurpation of poor parsons' earning (*GP* 442-44, 476, 334-54, 701-6). Narrators also disapprove more openly of, for example, the Summoner's craving for wine red as blood (*GP* 635). They seem less troubled by secular ethics, however, for they sound smugly amused that Manciple and Reeve cheat employers (*GP* 567-612). The narrators agree on most moral issues, that is, even without fusing into one narrating character.

ARGO, PLP 1002, record. Now available only as part of a two-cassette set (with *KnT*), SAY 91.

Chaucer. The Nun's Priest's Tale.

Readers John Burrow, Nevill Coghill, Lena Davis, Norman Davis.

1964 (cassette 1983).

The English Poets from Chaucer to Yeats, recorded in association with The British Council and Oxford University Press. Director George Rylands.

Side 1 (ARG 2743), band 1, *NPT* 2821-3000.
- band 2, *NPT* 3001-3109.
- band 3, *NPT* 3110-3186.
- band 4, *NPT* 3187-3266.

Side 2 (ARG 2744), band 1, *NPT* 3267-3374.
- band 2, *NPT* 3375-3446.
- band 3, *PLGW* G 1-78.
- band 4, *Truth*.
- band 5, *Lak*.
- band 6, *Bukton*.
- band 7, *Purse*.
- band 8, *Adam*.

Cover: Brief biography of Chaucer. Excerpt on *NPT* from Coghill's *The Poet Chaucer*. "The Pronunciation of Chaucer" by Norman Davis.

Enclosure (with the record): Eight-page booklet with all texts read, plus glosses. No credit given for edition or glosses. Line numbering is done for *NPT* beginning with line one, such that cuts are labelled lines 1-180, 181-289, and so on.

In the Argo interpretation of the frequently recorded *Nun's Priest's Tale*, the characters are consistent in their self-confidence and the narrator in his amusement. The smooth-talking fox is audibly untrustworthy, especially on "synge" in line 3290. Chaunticleer, unperturbed even in vulpine jaws, suggests a speech of defiance almost cheerfully, eager to convey his good idea and certain that his captor will succumb to the trick.

At line 3426 Chaunticleer even chuckles at his assured escape from the fox, as in line 2975 he chuckles at Pertelote's foolish belief in Cato. This latter responds in kind to Pertelote's near-chuckle at men's foolish belief in dreams of black devils (*NPT* 2936). Their marital relationship thus seems balanced, albeit not marked by sympathy for one another's shortcomings. Pertelote is quite matter-of-fact, for example, in stating that Chaunticleer's one instance of cowardice will end their lifetime together (*NPT* 2911). It is clear why Chaunticleer tolerates her too high expectations, however, for his voice bursts with affection while addressing her. Noting Andromache's status as "Ectores wyf," for example, his tone conveys "as you are mine, my dear" (*NPT* 3141).

Except for a tone of prayer to close, the narrator throughout sounds lightly amused at the concerns of animals. Starting each invocation with fake melodrama, he mocks literary conventions and thereby anyone moved by them (*NPT* 3226 ff., 3325 ff., 3338 ff.).

Among quite a few misprounced words, a correct ME "wydwe" in the first line is followed by one in which the final schwa tends toward ModE long *a*, as in the "narwe" two lines before it. Several ModE long *es* replace ME ones, as for "ye" in *NPT* 2926 and "she" in 2942, and a ModE "fellow" invades line 3086.

Fewer mispronunciations occur in the short poems, excepting a ModE "that" in *PLGW* G 41. These poems also permit less leeway in characterization. The *PLGW* narrator explains his fondness for books and daisies, serene and unimpetuous except for a hint on "delyte" that he might even like to eat them (G 30). The *Truth* narrator tends toward melodrama, with stretched verbs. He ignores the alleged "mede" pun in his fully sincere Envoy. A calmer narrator speaks with mild regret of the world's *Lak of Stedfastnesse*, indignation emerging only at line 21. Narrators directly address Bukton and Adam Scriveyn—the former kind, without overt joking, and the latter irritated but not one to compromise his dignity by scolding an employee. The empty purse is addressed in a steady tone of fake begging.

ARGO, ZPL 1003-4, two-record set. Now available only as two-cassette set, SAY 74.
Geoffrey Chaucer. Troilus and Criseyde.
Readers Derek Brewer, Richard Marquand, Peter Orr, Prunella Scales, Gary Watson.
1971 (cassette 1982).
The English Poets from Chaucer to Yeats, recorded in association with The British Council and Oxford University Press. Director George Rylands.
Record 1, side 1 (ZRG 3269), band 1, *Tr* 1.1-77, 85-161, 169-75, 183-96, 211-38, 267-87, 302-8, 379-92, 421-27, 547-74, 603-9, 701-7, 722-35, 750-63, 799-805, 862-82, 1058-64.
side 1, band 2, *Tr* 2.78-175, 183-217.
Record 1, side 2 (ZRG 3270), *Tr* 2.218-31, 239-336, 386-469, 498-525, 533-679, 764-924.
Record 2, side 1 (ZRG 3271), band 1, *Tr* 3.547-651, 687-707, 736-63, 939-80, 1051-57, 1086-1148, 1184-1211, 1247-67, 1317-23, 1709-29.
side 1, band 2, *Tr* 4.1-21, 659-72, 806-19, 939-59, 1086-99, 1107-27, 1247-53, 1275-81, 1415-21, 1688-1701.

Record 2, side 2 (ZRG 3272), *Tr* 5.1-28, 92-112, 176-82, 190-203, 771-77, 841-61, 869-75, 911-31, 1009-71, 1086-99, 1107-1218, 1226-32, 1744-71, 1786-1870.
Cover: Frontispiece to Corpus Christi ms. 61.
Enclosure (with the record): Fourteen-page booklet, with information about the performance; brief biography of Chaucer; excerpts on *Troilus* from books by Nevill Coghill, John Livingston Lowes, C. S. Lewis, and Derek Brewer; portrait of Troilus from Shakespeare's play; account of the ms. frontispiece reproduced on the cover, with credit to Cambridge University; and entire text read, plus glosses. No credit given for edition or glosses.

This recording effectively presents some highlights of *Troilus and Criseyde* as theater. It would be difficult to use with any edition of Chaucer other than its accompanying booklet, however, because the text skips unpredictably—a stanza here, a quarter book there—without warning.

The characterization of Criseyede is simplified. As "the ferfulleste wight," she fears love's changeability and even non-metaphorical rain (*Tr* 2.450, 771-805; 3.562). Otherwise she sounds eager from time to time; for example, she thinks her uncle really wants to know the plot of the book that she and her ladies are hearing (2.100-105). She sounds angry, too, at his treachery when he urges her to love Troilus before crow's feet appear (2.409-27).

Pandarus seems quite cruel to ignore her expressed objections so totally, in such a mean voice as his in 2.429-46. His sympathies are fully with Troilus throughout, not with his niece. Troilus, the weakest character, sounds passive even when evoking the gods en route to Criseyde's bedroom, such that Pandarus's enthusiastic scolding of his "wrecched mouses herte" seems overdone in contrast (3.712-36).

Unlike these three characters, the Argo narrator retains aloud the ambivalent attitude of Chaucer's textual narrator. Without overdoing disapproval, he spreads the blame around. In 1.183 Troilus is certainly setting himself up for a fall, according to the narrator's tone; and he and Pandarus are employing unethical tactics in 3.603. But Criseyde is not fully honest herself, as a pause conveys after 3.578, nor does she address the kneeling Troilus quite as chastely as she ought if she truly wished to discourage his attentions (3.972). While disapproving of her attraction to Diomede, the narrator also blames the Greek that she succumbs to his smooth blandishments (4.11, 5.854-63).

While censuring no character fully, the narrator reserves his fullest approval and affection for his little book itself (5.1786) and for its lessons that end Book 5. His closing attitude is consistent with the invocation to Book 1, wherein he settles happily into the role of storyteller (1.64). War and love make for a good story. If you have to frown and blame somebody at last, he suggests with a vocal shrug in 5.1845-55, why not blame the pagan gods and leave my wonderful fictional characters alone?

Pronunciation errors are sparse and not intrusive. In 1.109 "widewes" veers toward ModE "widow's," for example.

ARGO, ZPL 1008, record. No longer available in any form.
John Skelton and Early Lyric.
Readers David King, Yvonne Bonnamy, John Stride,
    Duncan McIntyre.
1971.

The English Poets from Chaucer to Yeats, recorded in association with The British Council.

Editions: (?) *Oxford Book of Scottish Verse*, ed. John MacQueen and Tom Scott (Oxford Clarendon); *Medieval English Lyrics*, ed. R. T. Davies (Faber & Faber).

Side 1 (ZRG 3363), Adam lay ibounden, Jesus woundes so wide, Of all wemen that ever were borne, I sing of a maiden, Com home againe, James I's *Kingis Quair*, Pleasure it is, Hay hay by this day, Now wolde I faine sum merthes make, I must go walke the woed so wild, In a goodly night as in my bede I laye, Here beside dwelleth a riche baron's doughter, I cannot eat but little meat.

Side 2 (ZRG 3364), John Skelton and other early modern writers.

Cover: Garden scene (from *Roman de la Rose*?) from unidentified B.L. ms. Commentary on Skelton by E. M. Forster and Peter Green, on medieval lyrics by E. K. Chambers, and on *Kingis Quair* by C. S. Lewis.

Enclosure: Twelve-page booklet with texts not credited, and glosses credited to MacQueen/Scott and Davies editions.

ARGO, ZPL 1208-10, three-record set. Now available only as part of a two-cassette set (with *NPT*), SAY 91.

Geoffrey Chaucer. The Knight's Tale.

Readers Richard Bebb, Frank Duncan, Peter Orr, Prunella Scales, Denis McCarthy, Roy Spencer.

1976 (cassette 1983).

Director Derek Brewer, producer Harley Usill, engineer Kevin Daly, editor Peter Orr. In association with The British Council.

"Recommended texts *The Knight's Tale*, ed. A. C. Spearing (Cambridge U. Press) and *Chaucer's Works*, ed. F. Robinson (Oxford U. Press)."
Side 1 (ZPL 1208/ ZRG 4443), *KnT* 859-1218.
Side 2 (ZPL 1208/ ZRG 4444), *KnT* 1219-1595.
Side 3 (ZPL 1209/ ZRG 4445), *KnT* 1596-1966.
Side 4 (ZPL 1209/ ZRG 4446), *KnT* 1967-2366.
Side 5 (ZPL 1210/ ZRG 4447), *KnT* 2367-2742.
Side 6 (ZPL 1210/ ZRG 4448), *KnT* 2743-3108.
Cover: Reproductions of Ellesmere ms. Knight and of a tournament from Harleian ms. 4431, fol. 150. Essay on *KnT* by Derek Brewer.

Herein most readers create characters consistent for the entire length of the *Knight's Tale*. The calm, dignified narrator, who must set the pace on this long journey, expresses interest in passing scenes but does not distract with melodrama or overexcitement. For example, he sounds rather angry when the boys fight like a tiger and lion, and thoughtful as he tries to recall exact political arrangements (*KnT* 1655 ff., 2970 ff.). With a professional storyteller's skill, he draws attention to certain lines by pausing after them. Thus a listener notices the foreshadowing in lines 1235 and 2564, or the odd detail of construction costs at line 2088.

Only occasionally does this narrator waver from cool professionalism; at line 2208 he seems peeved at, presumably, a restless audience. His irritation there is mild compared to Palamon and Arcite's throughout. As soon as they speak, even before Arcite sees Emelye and claims her too, it is clear that they have spent too much time together, have gotten on each other's nerves often before now. A very sarcastic "leeve brother" at line 1136 is not being uttered in that tone for the first time. This oral interpretation has not been proposed in criticism but is true to the text which says just that the two were cousins, not that they ever liked each other. In all their exchanges throughout the Tale, the Argo pair snarl pure resentment. Tattletale Palamon gloats with joy at the chance to condemn Arcite, who on his deathbed will pass the girl to Palamon only in a Christianlike hope of saving his own soul, not from any regret or belief that his cousin is in fact "worthy to ben loved" (*KnT* 1724, 2794).

Being only a pawn in their game, Emelye delivers a memorized prayer as her only speech. A motherly Diana replies. The other deities also project distinct characters: Mars ghoulish, Venus spoiled, her father Saturn kind and indulgent (*KnT* 2297-2330, 2348-57, 2433, 2667, 2453-78, 2668-70). One other character, minor in the text, stands out in performance because of oral contrast both with Emelye and with their sovereign. When Theseus meets the weeping company of black-clad ladies and furiously demands that they let go of his bridle and shut up, the "eldeste lady" does not cower or whine or beg mercy. Instead, she states their problem with dignified authority (*KnT* 905 ff.)

In contrast to her cool-headedness, the Argo Theseus loses his temper too abruptly for the text to support. His rage is more justifiable toward unsupervised fighting or his servant's disguise than toward ladies in mourning, although in neither case is anger a necessary response (*KnT* 1712, 1743-47). Immediately, though, Theseus shifts moods so totally that his amused, genial account of hot lovers seems to emit from somebody else (*KnT* 1785 ff.). At times his excessive anger creates new, viable textual possibilities. By sounding peeved and dissatisfied when he closes the lists at line 2656, for example, Theseus seems to have hoped all along that Palamon would win.

Throughout the recording recur some pronunciation errors—not too intrusive, however, because of their consistency. The ModE cognate is nearly always substituted for ME "heigh," "though," "and," and "to," along with isolated ModE instances such as "he" in *KnT* 894. In addition, the readers often slide a final *e* toward a ModE long-*a* sound—thus "sorway" for "sorwe," "widway" for "wydwe," "strokays" for "strokes," and so on (*KnT* 951, 1359, 2822, 1171, 1922). They also substitute ModE "nay" for ME "ne" throughout lists of negatives (*KnT* 1941-45, 2543-48, 2920-62).

ARGO, ZPL 1211, record. Now available only as part of a two-cassette set (with *GP*), SAY 24.
Geoffrey Chaucer. *The Pardoner's Tale.*
Readers Frank Duncan, Peter Orr, Roy Spencer, Richard Bebb.
1976 (cassette 1982).
Director Derek Brewer, producer Harley Usill, editor Peter Orr, engineer Kevin Daly. In association with The British Council.
"Recommended texts *The Pardoner's Tale*, ed. A. C. Spearing (Cambridge U. Press) and *Chaucer's Works*, ed. F. Robinson (Oxford U. Press)."
Side 1, band 1, *PardT* 329-462.
    band 2, *PardT* 463-660.
Side 2, *PardT* 661-968.
Cover: Brief introduction to *CT*, the Pardoner as character, his Tale, and ME pronunciation. Portrait of Chaucer from B.L. Add. ms. 5141.

Exploiting to the fullest the possibilities in Chaucer's text, this performance provides yet another explanation—more compelling than many in print—for the Pardoner's charm that can overwhelm gullible churchgoers and wary pilgrims alike. By bringing out comic strains in the sermon, the Argo reader draws listeners to see the world through the Pardoner's eyes, as a mass of stupid people ripely deserving trickery. For example, *PardT* 554-55 may not seem side-splittingly funny on paper but aloud become so, as this reader pinches his nostrils to emit "Sampsoun, Sampsoun" as open-mouthed drunken snores. Knowing full well that his ignorant church audience will never notice the total irrelevance of this point, this Pardoner delivers "and yet, God woot, Sampsoun drank nevere no wyn" with fullscale preacherly indignation. High-blown indignation is likewise directed at such targets as cooks cooking, wine so bad that the drinker is transported to Spain, and the possible confusion of Lamuel with Samuel (*PardT* 538-46, 565-71, 585). Subtly, like the wine of Spain itself, this Pardoner's mockery creeps into a listener's consciousness and eases the conscience. It gradually becomes quite all right to laugh at and thereby, eventually, to cheat the uneducated.

Thus, this oral Pardoner does what reader-response critics claim as value in the greatest literature on paper: he lures a listener into the text's moral dilemmas. Elsewhere, while remaining separated from his attitudes, listeners can still appreciate how his shifting tones of voice emerge from a consistent personality. He begins in a gentle, gleefully sinister tone, confident and self-satisfied as he shares the secrets of his trade. He sounds evil when he speaks of the church (e.g., *PardT* 421-22), but less wicked than determined at line 453, as if he has set a personal goal of one wench per town.

This Pardoner delivers the much-discussed benediction, *PardT* 916-18, with studied casualness. He pretends to hesitate, as if troubled not by the pardons' potential effectiveness but only by the propriety of sales during a social occasion.

With a chuckle at line 942, then, he tries to draw the Host into the swindle: "Hey, pretend you're buying a pardon, ok?" The Host starts to joke back, but from line 952 on becomes more and more angry—perhaps at his own ethical lapse.

Within the Tale told by this complex yet consistent Pardoner, characterization is less compelling than for its teller. The riotours and the old man sound equal in sedate dignity, at times, but at other times convey attitudes not quite compatible with that one. For example, the first riotour solemnly rallies his friends to go seek Death. Yet when he addresses the old man, shortly thereafter, he responds to hearty friendliness with unmotivated spite (*PardT* 692-701, 715-19). The old man remains sedate, though. He firmly lectures these insolent teenagers, slightly irritated but not shaken by their behavior. When they reply with more insolence, he looses his ultimate weapon in satisfied tones. His closing line 767 sounds as hearty as did his greeting, but he chuckles in happy anticipation of their well-deserved deaths.

This old man's parting chuckle is not so overtly sinister as are some chuckles by this Pardoner himself. Or is it? At any rate, this album's subtle unity and complexity both, in its projection of Chaucer's versatile text, more than compensates for relatively frequent misprouciations. The slips become intrusive in that two dropped syllables affect meter: "hadde" in *PardT* 707 and "botelles" in 871 each lacks a syllable. Otherwise, a few final schwas edge toward ModE long *a,* including "othes" as if "othays" in 659; and some words resemble too closely their ModE cognates. Most of these latter are small words like "be" and "to" and "that," except for a ModE "devil's" for "develes" in 470, and a ModE "precious" in 775.

ARGO, (Z)RG (5)443, record.
Medieval English Lyrics.
Performers Grayston Burgess, Gerald English, John F. Frost, Owen Grundy, Robin Stenham, Robert Tear, John Whitworth, Osian Ellis, Desmond Dupré, Joan Rimmer, Christopher Taylor, Christopher Wellington.
1965.
Editors/directors Frank L1. Harrison and Eric J. Dobson. In association with The British Council.
Edition: E.J. Dobson and Frank L1. Harrison, *Medieval English Songs* (Faber & Faber).
Side 1 (ZRG 2719), Perspice christicola/Sumer is icumen in, Fuweles in the frith, Sainte Marie Virgine, Miri it is, Gabriel fram heven-king, Stond wel moder under rode, Nowel nowel nowel.
Side 1 (ZRG 2720), Deo gracias Anglie/Owr king went forth, Pray for us thou prince of pes, Go hert hurt with adversitee, Now wold y fayn, This day day daws, Green growith th'holy.
Cover: Reading Rota ms.
Enclosure: Eight-page booklet with introduction by E. J. Dobson and his texts and glosses or translation of each, credited.

BELLEROPHON, no number, floppy record.
Chaucer Coloring Book.
Reader Charles Muscatine.
1979.
ISBN #0-88388-017-2.
Side 1, *GP* 1-46, 118-62, 165-72.
Side 2, *GP* 285-308, 331-40, 379-95, 545-66, 751-72.

Enclosures: Text of entire *GP* from one of Skeat's editions, although the reading-aloud is from Robinson's. The coloring book consists of reproductions (not easily available elsewhere) of woodcut pilgrims from the editions of William Caxton (1484?), Wynkyn de Worde (1494), and Richard Pynson (1526), along with other woodcut scenes such as the pilgrims at table. On the covers are portraits of Chaucer from the Ellesmere ms. and Corpus Christi ms. 61. Credit given for all pictures but not for the edition.

Fading into and out of Renaissance-style flute music, a bemused narrator genially advises us of some morally insignificant shortcomings of characters who go on so-called "pilgrimages," his voice inserting these ironic quotation marks into *GP* 12. After a tone of warning throughout the long "whan" clause, he shifts to eagerness to share his experiences by line 20, then pride in his ability to make friends by 31-32. At 38-39 he seems to address children, the presumed audience for a Chaucer coloring book.

Among the five pilgrim portraits presented full-length, the Prioress and Clerk are the most colored by the narrator's amused sympathy at minor foibles. Gentle chuckles convey this attitude at *GP* 136, 148, 150, 156, 288, and 296. The other three pilgrims, Cook and Miller and Host, sound heartier. The narrator tends to imitate each pilgrim's own voice rather than convey his own attitude toward them, except for a vocal shrug—"Who am I to say anything bad about gold thumbs?"— on *GP* 563. Slips in pronunciation occur as ModE "made" for "maad" in line 394, and as ModE rather than French *us* in "vertu," "aventure," and "cure" (*GP* 4, 25, 303).

CAEDMON, TC 1008, record. Now available only as cassette, SWC 1008.
Chaucer. The Canterbury Tales. The Nun's Priest's Tale. The Pardoner's Prologue and Tale.
Reader Robert Ross.
1956 (orig. 1953).
L. of C. #RA55-275.
Side 1, *PardT* 329-528, 660-945.
Side 2, *NPT* 2821-3446.
Cover: Brief essay on Middle English, with gratuitous apology for lapses in the ME prounciation of "the late Robert Ross, no scholar but an actor well-known for his roles in such plays as...."
Enclosure (with the record): Sixteen-page booklet with texts read. No credit given for edition.

Though not quite so complex in characterization as some other recordings of these frequently anthologized Tales, the Caedmon renderings combine professional acting techniques with full awareness of standard critical issues. In the *Nun's Priest's Tale*, for example, an extremely noble and dignified Chaunticleer confides fear to his wife; with exasperated dignity, then, he replies to her increasingly peevish demands that he take laxatives so as to remain her hero (*NPT* 2892-2907, 2970 ff.). The cock's self-confidence falters, however, in the totally unprecedented situation of being borne away on a fox's back. He speaks up a bit scared, unsure that his plan will work ... and, in a masterstroke of dramatization, lines 3407-13 are performed through a clutched throat.

In the other Tale, the Caedmon Pardoner seizes gleefully on the chance to tell all, breaking into fiendish cackles from time to time (e.g., *PardT* 365, 371, 406, 442). His sinister tones concerning his own work, especially at any instance of the word "holy," echo the tones of characters in his Tale. Some seem problematic. Should the old man sound quite so gleeful when he points the riotours toward the death trap, or the apothecary quite so villainous while selling rat poison (*PardT* 760-67, 859-67)? Each sinister tone does differ, though, and the riotours' characterization remains strikingly consistent. They are repulsive slobs from their first crude demands to the boy (*PardT* 667) to their closing plan to bury the body of the youngest, probably after gleefully mutilating it (*PardT* 884).

After his Tale, even such a fiendish Pardoner as this cannot ignore half a century of scholarly commentary as to the exact vocal shade of genuine or pretended sincerity or insincerity concerning Christ's pardon. He stumbles and misreads line 918 as "I wol nat yow deceyve," then corrects it to "yow nat" before launching into a chuckling, teasing sales pitch to the pilgrims. No longer so sinister, the Pardoner seems boyishly pleased at holding the center of attention. Satisfied that his show will continue thereby, he urges the Host to unbuckle his purse (*PardT* 945). To any listener's disappointment, the Caedmon reading ends right there. No Host replies.

The reader makes a few minor pronunciation errors. He sometimes gives a ME long-*i* value to short *i*s, as for "Latyn," "mystriste," and "wiste" (*PardT* 344, 369-70), and he veers toward ModE pronunciation on a few phrases, including "shal have" and "whoso" (*PardT* 383-85). Medievalists who think that they remember the pronunciation as faulty should re-listen. They are remembering the record-cover apology rather than the performance itself.

CAEDMON, TC 1021, record. Now available only as cassette, SWC 1021.
Hearing Poetry. Volume One: Chaucer through Milton.

Reader Frank Silvera.
1960.
Narrator Mark Van Doren, director Howard O. Sackler.
Readers other than for Chaucer, Hurd Hatfield and Jo Van Fleet.
L. of C. #RA55-196.
Side 1, band 1, *PLGW* F 1-8, G 29-50.
  bands 2-7, Selections from Spenser, Marlowe, Dekker, and Shakespeare.
Side 2, bands 1-5, Selections from Jonson, Donne, Herbert, and Milton.
Cover: Purpose in making the recorded anthology.
Enclosure (with the record): Six-page booklet with all texts read. No editions credited.

If "courtly love" were an audible sound, not an abstract scholarly construct, it would sound like these lines G 29-50. (The effect is less noticeable for *PLGW* F 1-8, read first in a gently explanatory tone and followed by paraphrases.) A "courtly-love" tone mixes breathless religious awe with sexual anticipation, the latter particularly audible on "delyte" (G 30) and building toward trembling eagerness at G 45 ff. Since the stated objects of the narrator's awe and affection, books and daisies, have little literal connection to religion or to sex, one can ponder the extent to which the entire metaphorical relationship can be made manifest in performance.

Pronunciation slides toward ModE from time to time, as on "love" and "dayesyes" (G 42-43). A few vowels are off kilter in other ways; for instance, "helle" in F 2 resembles ModE "hail" plus schwa.

CAEDMON, SWC 1030, cassette.
Wellsprings of Drama.
Frank Silvera and others, reading mostly Modern English.
1957?
Director Howard Sackler.
L. of C. #R57-1200.
Quem Quaeritis; Banns; ModE translations of The Deluge, Robin Hood and the Friar, and Abraham and Isaac.

Only the banns are in Middle English.

CAEDMON, SWC 1031, cassette.
Everyman.
Readers Burgess Meredith and others.
1957?
Director Howard Sackler.
L. of C. #RA57-106.
Entire play.

CAEDMON, SWC 1032, cassette.
The Second Sheperd's [sic] *Play.*
Joss Ackland and others, reading Modern English from an unidentified translation.
1966?
Director Howard Sackler.
L. of C. #R66-1757.

Not in Middle English.

CAEDMON, SWC 1054, cassette.
The Cambridge Treasury of English Prose: Malory to Donne.
Readers Cambridge University members.
1957?
L. of C. #RA57-253.
Excerpts from Thomas Malory's *Morte d'Arthur*; early modern writers.

CAEDMON, TC 1102, record. Now available only as cassette, SWC 1102.
Chaucer. The Canterbury Tales. The Wife of Bath's Prologue. The Wife of Bath's Tale.
Dame Peggy Ashcroft, reading Modern English from J. U. Nicholson's translation.
1961.
L. of C. #R61-1759.

Not in Middle English.

CAEDMON, TC 1130, record. Now available only as cassette, SWC 1130.
Chaucer. The Canterbury Tales. The Miller's Tale and the Pardoner's Tale.
Stanley Holloway and Micheal MacLiammóir, reading Modern English from Theodore Morrison's translation.
1963.
L. of C. #R66-1803.

Not in Middle English.

CAEDMON, TC 1151, record. Also available as cassette, CDL5 1151.
The Canterbury Tales. Chaucer. General Prologue. Prologue to the Parson's Tale. The Retraction.
Reader Jess B. Bessinger, Jr.
1962.
L. of C. #R65-999.
Side 1, *GP* 1-476.
Side 2, *GP* 477-858, *ParsP* 1-74, *Retraction.*
Cover: Essay by Bessinger on Chaucer's oral context and style, keyed to these specific readings.
Enclosure (with the record): Twelve-page booklet with texts read, credited to F. N. Robinson and Houghton Mifflin.

A wide range of subtly distinguished attitudes toward the various pilgrims emanates from a consistently characterized pilgrim/narrator. This narrator genially accepts imperfection in the people he meets, but is not fooled by surface appearances. His voice doubts, for example, that the Knight's love of "trouthe and honour" fully accounts for his life's activities (*GP* 46). Although the narrator is old enough to chuckle at the Squire's youthfulness (*GP* 92), he has not experienced all of life. Only after a thoughtful, almost puzzled listing of accoutrements does he come to realize that what he sees before him must be a "forster" (*GP* 117). And he has never been to sea, certainly never been brought safely to shore in a storm thanks to another's skill, for he finds the Shipman's knowledge petty and insignificant (*GP* 401-10).

During his life on dry land, mostly in town, the narrator seems to have had bad experiences with doctors and lawyers. The Physician's knowledge sounds as empty as the Shipman's, as each professional's portrait becomes a gleeful frame for its pomposity-deflating line (*GP* 322, 444). The narrator has apparently had good experiences with hardheaded millers, though, for he describes this one with relish (*GP* 561-62). Likewise, he sounds satisfied at the Manciple's ability to cheat so many learned men (*GP* 573-75, 586). Although he thus sees little value in theoretical legal knowledge, he does approve of the Monk's practical use of booklearning and rhetorical skills. All in all, the narrator judges people as individuals, not by absolute standards of right and wrong.

Much Chaucer criticism has treated the relationship between the *General Prologue* narrator and Chaucer himself. Many scholars—not all— believe that the *Retraction* to the *Canterbury Tales* expresses the genuine attitudes of Chaucer-the-man. The Caedmon reading of the *Retraction* well exemplifies the text's potential to remain ambiguous even when interpreted aloud. The kind and humble speaker slows down and speaks more softly as he approaches the end of the list of worldly writings for which he seeks forgiveness. A long pause after "many a leccherous lay" could convey sincere regret for the sin, or else regret that lays constitute sin, or else nostalgic reminiscence, or almost as many other attitudes as the text on paper would allow.

In the *Retraction* occur occasional ModE pronunciations of "me." The only intrusive one is in line 1084, "foryeve me my giltes," wherein both pronouns sound alike.

CAEDMON, SWC 1161, cassette.
Beowulf and Other Poetry (in Old English).
Reader Jess B. Bessinger, Jr.
1966?
L. of C. #R66-1802.

Caedmon's Hymn, Dream of the Rood, Wanderer, Battle of Brunanburh, Wife's Lament; *Beowulf* 1-125, 195-225, 702-852, 3137-3180.

CAEDMON, TC 1192, record. Now available only as cassette, SWC 1192.
[Dialogues from] Gawain and the Green Knight and the Pearl.
Readers Jess B. Bessinger, Jr., Marie Borroff.
1965.
L. of C. #R66-1801.
Editions: *SGGK*, ed. Israel Gollancz, with Mabel Day and M. S. Serjeantson (London: for E.E.T.S. by Oxford Univ. Press, 1940); *Pearl*, ed. E. V. Gordon (Oxford: Clarendon, 1953).
Side 1, band 1, *SGGK* 1126-1318.
    band 2, *SGGK* 1421-1557.
    band 3, *SGGK* 1690-1921.
Side 2, *Pearl* 1-72, 121-32, 157-68, 181-92, 229-468, 709-852, 865-924, 937-96.
Cover: Stylized beheading scene. Essay on the two poems by Bessinger and Borroff.
Enclosure: 24-page booklet with texts credited, and translations by Borroff.

CAEDMON, SWC 1223, cassette.
Chaucer. Two Canterbury Tales. The Miller's Tale and the Reeve's Tale.
Reader Jess B. Bessinger, Jr.
1972.

L. of C. #R67-2715.
Side 1, *MlrT* 3109-3686 (31 min., 44 sec.).
Side 2, *MlrT* 3687-3854, *RvT* 3855-4324 (34:50).
Cover: Essay by Bessinger on Chaucer's fabliaux, keyed to these specific readings. Inaccurate timings for Prologues and Tales separately, listing them as if the entire *MlrT* fit on Side 1.

In these two Tales, characters and pilgrim tellers alike are effectively projected. In the Prologue to the *Miller's Tale*, for example, a clear distinction is audible among attitudes toward the Miller's inebriated state. The narrator sedately disapproves; the Host is kind and indulgent toward a good customer; the Reeve snorts with disdain.

The Miller himself blubbers line 3132, but then takes control of his voice enough to advise the Reeve (*MlrT* 3151-66) and to tell his entire Tale consistently in the voice of a red-faced gulping drunk. He is sober enough, however, to convey double entendres. He spotlights not only the famous pun at *MlrT* 3275-76, but also an unremarked possibility whereby Nicholas's offer to share with John a "certeyn thyng that toucheth me and thee" can refer to Alisoun as well as to the prophecy (*MlrT* 3494).

The *Reeve's Tale* is not so surely told in the Reeve's own voice, although the whining self-pity of his Prologue is consistent with his self-satisfied indignation at the behavior of the Symkyns. Instead, the narrator participates in the story. For example, in bed the clerks whisper so as not to wake the snoring family. The narrator whispers also, as if he were crouched in the darkened room ready to describe the action (*RvT* 4169-98).

Pronunciation is correct throughout. At about twenty lines occur the vocal equivalent of scribal errors. For example, Absolon will tell Gerveys why he wants the hot poker "another day," not the text's "to-morwe day" (*M1rT* 3784), and Aleyn invokes the legal reprisal for having had an "il fit al today" rather than the text's "this day" (*RvT* 4184). Some of these variants very closely resemble those of scribes, in that they substitute for Northern and obsolete forms their synonyms that have survived into ModE, such as "I" for "ik," "poore" for "povre," and "lost" for "lorn" (*RvT* 3888, 4002, 4073).

CAEDMON, TC 1226, record. Now available only as cassette, SWC 1226.
The Poetry of Chaucer. The Parliament of Fowls and Six Lyric Poems.
Reader Jess B. Bessinger, Jr.
1967?
L. of C. #R67-3730.
E. Talbot Donaldson, ed., *Chaucer's Poetry: An Anthology for the Modern Reader* (New York: Ronald Press, 1958).
Side 1, *PF* 1-483 (28 min., 47 sec.).
Side 2, band 1, *PF* 484-699 (12:28).
    band 2, *Merciles Beaute* (2:30).
    band 3, *To Rosemounde* (1:32).
    band 4, *Lak* (including envoy to Richard II) (1:45).
    band 5, *Purse* (including envoy to Henry IV) (1:38).
    band 6, *Adam* (0:28).
    band 7, *Scogan* (3:10).
Cover: Essay by Bessinger on these specific poems.
Enclosure (with the record): 32-page booklet with texts read plus glosses, credited to E. Talbot Donaldson and the Ronald Press. Passages are given above exactly as printed on the album and booklet covers, and as

performed. However, no text is included for the envoys that end *Lak* and *Purse*; and the birds' song printed in the booklet differs slightly both from Donaldson's edition and from the recorded performance of *PF* 680-92.

This recording seems hastily produced. The texts enclosed do not align exactly with those performed, and *Parliament of Fowls* is not as fully dramatized as its multitude of voices on the page would allow. The narrator is fond of books every time he says the word, but otherwise wavers in his character. He disapproves of Beute's lack of attire in line 225, for example, but changes to gusto concerning Venus's lack of attire, leaving a long pause after line 273 to force the listener to picture her thus.

Other characters likewise vacillate in their attitudes, or display bland ones. Scipio Affrican is sometimes evil and sometimes a doomsayer (*PF* 52, 80). Nature does remain a smooth professional throughout. The goose and duck are peasants, similar in tone. The cuckoo sounds a bit sinister. Of the three tercels, only the middle one has a distinct character, that of a rough soldier. Line 540, with which they could all three leap to their clawed feet drawing swords with wings, is disappointingly neutral.

A few lapses into ModE occur—"be" in *PF* 264, for example. A textual variant in line 439 reduces to three the number of negatives with which the first tercelet vows service.

Of the short poems, only *Purse* sounds at all cheerful. Otherwise, the literary genre "complaint" conveys resentful complaining. The narrator of *Merciles Beaute* does not want to be slain, even metaphorically, and resents the pain already suffered. The elderly man complaining about the world's lack of steadfastness waxes indignant at times, especially in the second stanza. The firm scolder of Adam Scriveyn is not amused.

CAEDMON, SWC 1374, cassette.
Morte d'Arthur.
Reader Siobhan McKenna.
1975?
L. of C. #75-752655.
Excerpts from different sections of Thomas Malory's work, assembled to trace the story of Launcelot and Guenever with intervening quests and combats.

CAEDMON, SWC 1424, cassette.
Kemp Malone on Old English.
Reader Kemp Malone.
1973?
L. of C. #73-750640.
Earth Mother of Men, Dream of the Rood, Genesis B (Satan's Speech to His Followers), Wife's Lament, Wulf and Eadwacer, Battle of Maldon (i.e.?, The Fall of the Earl of Essex), Wanderer; Malone's ModE translations of some or all.

CAEDMON, CDL5 3008 or SWC 3008, three-cassette set.
Also available as three-record set, TC 3008.
A History of the English Language.
Reader Jess B. Bessinger, Jr.
1973.

Co-ordinator Diane Bornstein.
L. of C. #73-750641.
Side 1, Introduction, Caedmon's Hymn, *Beowulf* 1-52, Alfred's Preface to Pope Gregory's *Pastoral Care* (19 min., 40 sec.).
Side 2, Aelfric's Homily on St. Gregory the Great, Wulfstan's *Sermo ad Anglos*, Anglo-Saxon Chronicles (for the years 449, 601, 991, 1017, 1066, 1137, 1154), Layamon's *Brut, Ancrene Riwle*, Alysoun (22:25).
Side 3, Dan Michel's *Ayenbite of Inwyt*, Robert Mannyng's *Story of Englande, GP* 1-42, *Astr* 1-49, Richard Rolle's *Bee and the Stork, Sir Gawain and the Green Knight* 670-712 (20:46).
Side 4, Thomas Malory's *Book of King Arthur*, William Caxton's Prologue to *Eneydos*; selections from early Modern English (24:08).
Sides 5 and 6, Selections from the sixteenth through eighteenth centuries.
Cover: Besides its own contents, with separate timings but without line numbers, each of the three cassettes provides the same short introduction to the history of English and a list of credits for editions, excluding Chaucer. The tapes accompany *In Forme of Speche is Chaunge*, ed. John H. Fisher and Diane Bornstein (Englewood Cliffs, N.J.: Prentice-Hall, 1974).
Enclosure: Text of all readings, also available separately as TTC 3008.

A concise account of each work of literature, its dialect, and its place in linguistic development introduces each selection. In most cases the excerpt begins at the beginning of the work; this discography supplies line number only for the most commonly anthologized works (Chaucer's, *Beowulf, SGGK*).

The introduction to the *GP* excerpt draws attention to the French and Latin loan words in the opening lines, rather than to its literary setting. Accordingly the reading is didactic rather than dramatic, in a tone of importance merging toward warning, until a thoughtful narrator enters at line 19. The pilgrims sound jolly (*GP* 24-29), and the narrator takes pride in his journalistic ability (*GP* 32, 40-41).

"Ability" is one of occasional ModE cognates that have crept into this reading of *Treatise on the Astrolabe*, along with "instrument" twice (*Astr* 2, 13, 17). This passage's didactic tone, though not gripping, does enact the text. The narrator raises his voice at *Astr* 19-24, for example, perhaps because little Lowys has begun to squirm.

CAEDMON, TC 4001, four-record set. Also available as
    four cassettes, CDL5 4001.
Beowulf (in Old English).
Reader Kemp Malone.
1967?
L. of C. #R67-3202.
Entire poem.

CAMBRIDGE, cassette. No longer available in any form.
*Selected Tales from Chaucer. The Merchant's Prologue and
    Tale.*
Reader A. C. Spearing.
1976.
ISBN #521 21187 5, VAT #214 1416 14.
Maurice Hussey, ed., *The Merchant's Prologue and Tale*
    (Cambridge: Cambridge UP, 1966).

Side 1, *GP* 273-86, *McfT* 1213-1865 (35 min.).
Side 2, *McfT* 1866-2440 (30 min.).
Available copy not audible.
Special Note: Cambridge University Press has discontinued this series of tapes made to accompany editions of individual Tales. The Press claims to have kept no information whatsoever, even as to which Tale was read by whom. From older publicity material, it appears that Elizabeth Salter read *WBP* and *WBT*, and A. C. Spearing *MlrT*; possibly the *Clerk's Tale* was recorded also.

CAPITOL, SW 229, record. No longer available in any form.
The Canterbury Tales: A Musical.
Modern English from translation by Nevill Coghill and Martin Starkie. Music by Richard Hill and John Hawkins.
1969.

Not in Middle English.

CASSETTE BOOK COMPANY, 853, two-cassette set.
Tales of Chaucer / Chaucer's Canterbury Tales.
Bob French, reading Modern English from an unidentified translation of *MLT, WBT, ClT, McfT, FrkT, CYT*, and *PardT*.

Not in Middle English.

COLUMBIA, AMS 6198, record.
Lester Trimble. Four Fragments from the Caunterbury Tales.
Performer Adele Addison.
1958.
Columbia Records Collector's Series. Modern American Music Series. Musicians Robert Conant, Charles Russo, Martin Orenstein.
L. of C. #R60-1345.
Apparently an adaptation of one of W. W. Skeat's editions.
Side 1 (XMS 51046), band 1, *GP* 1-11, 19-32, 36-39a.
  band 2, *GP* 42-50, 68-72, 75-78.
  band 3, *GP* 80-84, 89-95a, 97-98.
  band 4, *WBP* 1-5a, 6, 8-10, 13, 15-19, 21-23, 28-34.
  (Line repetitions and word inversions are not noted here.)
Side 2, Music unrelated to Chaucer: *Theodore Chanler. Nine Epitaphs.*
Cover: Biography of Trimble, and an account of how he came to compose the piece. Autobiography and account by Chanler.

This item features excerpts from *Canterbury Tales* sung, accompanied principally by harpsichord. The soprano pronounces ME correctly; at *WBP* 31 she starts to sing a ModE "me," but then adjusts its vowel to ME while holding the note.

The musical settings are appropriate, if somewhat clichéd. During *GP* 75-78, for example, with a sort of hobby-horse trot on the harpsichord the Knight rides off into the sunset at the end of a cowboy movie. The Squire is interpreted with effects of Renaissance flute dance. The Wife of Bath emerges a tortured figure. Jesus speaks *WBP* 17-19 amidst music of gloom and foreboding; the Wife's refutation of his words sounds shaky, not at all confident, because sung to nervous, confused, driving instrumentation.

DECCA, DL 9418, record. Availability not checked.
Medieval English Carols and Italian Dances.
Performers Ronald Roseman, Charles Bressler, Robert White, Gordon Myers, Arthur Burrows, John Ferrante, Brayton Lewis, Sheila Schonbrun, David Dodds, Marvin Hayes (i.e., New York Pro Musica).
1962.
Director Noah Greenberg.
L. of C. #R62-1209.
Side 1 (MG 8502), Two Italian instrumentals; Nowel syng we bothe al and som, Lullay lullay, Ave Maria gracia dei plena, Ther is no rose, Ave rex angelorum, Nova nova.
Side 2 (MG 8503), Two Italian instrumentals; Latin song; Make we joye nowe in this fest, Hayl Mary ful of grace, Mervele noght Joseph on Mary mylde, Nowell nowell nowell, The Agincourt Carol.
Cover: Dancers from unidentified ms.
Enclosure: Three-page booklet with introduction, texts, and translations, not credited.

DEUTSCHE GRAMMOPHON, 139380, record.
The Canterbury Pilgrims: A Description in Words and Music.
Martin Starkie, reading Modern English adapted by Nevill Coghill from his translation. Music composed and arranged by John Hawkins and Richard Hill, and performed by The Gabrieli Brass.
1960s.

Not in Middle English.

EAV, KE 0296, cassette. Not available as record, LE 7733B.
The Time, Life, and Works of Geoffrey Chaucer / The Tale of the Wyf of Bathe.
Reader Norman Davis.
1968.
Editor Hilary Reid, research assistant Gillian de Mariassy.
L. of C. #FiA 68-4277.
Side 1, Introduction (read by Bryan Kendrick) to medieval love as "an art to be learned and practiced," including ME rendering of *WBP* 1-8; plot summary of *WBT*; *WBT* 857-1133, 1150-64, 1177-90, 1207-64 (25 min., 25 sec.).
Side 2, Blank.
Enclosures: This cassette is one of two that accompany EAV's filmstrip B7KF 0068, with the same main title. The other cassette contains a narration by Peter Howell, coordinated with the filmstrip, for manual projectors on one side and automatic on the other. (The *WBT*, which originally filled the second side of the one record in the kit, is not coordinated with the filmstrip.) Two booklets are included. In the four-page Teacher's Notes, along with suggestions for classroom use, is reproduced the frame-by-frame narration for 47 scenes from medieval manuscripts (only the Ellesmere being identified). The ten-page Study Guide provides a one-page introduction to Chaucer's times and the *WBT*; the entire text of the *WBT* (with brackets around portions not read aloud); a glossary divided into "recurring" and "nonrecurring" words; and a chronology of Chaucer's life. Multiple

copies available of Study Guide, in sets of 35 only, as stock number B9BB 0997. No credit given for edition.

This performance conveys what is emphasized in the recording's introduction: the Tale is a vehicle for the character of its narrator, Alysoun of Bath. Her personality bubbles up, for example, in delight at mention of widows. At both lines 1027 and 1044, she seems to be waving eagerly and pointing at herself—"Yoo hoo! A wise widow! That's moi!" In addition, she certainly teases the Friar with lines 873-81; she utters with anticipatory relish the term "lusty bacheler," brags that women don't keep secrets, and closes in a jovial tone of pretended indignation (*WBT* 883, 950, 1261-64). Throughout the Tale, the only stretch not fully Wife of Bathian is the opening, wherein the speaker seems to be mocking superstitious peasants.

The characters in the Tale likewise sport appropriate voices. Among female speakers, the kindly queen has low expectations: she has assigned this same task before (*WBT* 902-12). Midas's wife runs the gamut of emotions in her few lines. She pleads with the water at line 974 and heaves a sigh after 976, then speeds up to a glad lilt. The old hag is in charge at all times. She orders the knight to halt; later she announces her intended marriage, knowing just how he will respond (*WBT* 1001-4, 1055-57). Her coyness and implied pouting in bed sound equally self-assured (*WBT* 1236-37).

Characterization wavers somewhat for the male protagonist. Nonetheless, the knight's attitudes form a possible succession: heartiness on pledging his trouthe to the hag, confidence while addressing the court, unsurprised sadness on hearing his wife-to-be's statement thereof, and calm acceptance of her sovereignty (*WBT* 1013, 1037-42, 1058-61, 1238). In all these moods, the knight seems untroubled by female superiority.

It is only a certain untroubledness throughout that keeps this on the lesser side of the line between a good performance and a great performance—a certain calmness of narration that keeps this just a story, not an event. Pronunciation slips are sparse and slight: a ModE "we" in line 1260, for example, and ModE "that" twice (*WBT* 1019, 1251).

EAV, LE 7650-55, two-record set. Also B9RR 0937.
A Thousand Years of English Pronunciation.
Reader Helge Kökeritz.
1961.
L. of C. #R64-930.
F. N. Robinson, ed., *The Complete Works of Geoffrey Chaucer* (Boston: Houghton Mifflin, 1933), but with spelling variants.
Record 1, side 1, band 1, *Beowulf* 205-28.
   band 2, *Beowulf* 405-32.
   band 3, *Beowulf* 2801-20.
   band 4, *Beowulf* 3156-82.
   band 5, Aelfric's Homily, The Assumption of St. John.
   band 6, Anglo-Saxon Gospel, Luke 7.2-9.
   band 7, Wyclif-Purvey translation, Luke 7.2-9.
   band 8, Authorized Version of 1611, Luke 7.2-9.
Record 1, side 2, band 1, The Cuckoo Song (Sumer is icumen in).
   band 2, *Piers Plowman* B 1-27.
   band 3, A Moral Tale in Fourteenth-Century Kentish.
   band 4, *Sir Gawain and the Green Knight* 37-59.

band 5, John of Trevisa's Account of the Languages of Britain.
band 6, *GP* 445-76.
band 7, *GP* 477-500.
band 8, *GP* 822-56.
band 9, *Tr* 3.1079-1141.
Record 2, side 1, William Caxton's Prologue to *Eneydos*; selections from Wyatt, Spenser, and Shakespeare.
Record 2, side 2, Selections from the late sixteenth century, the seventeenth century, and Pope.
Cover: Biography and publications of Kökeritz.
Enclosures: Sixteen-page booklet outlining history of English (including Great Vowel Shift) and introducing the works excerpted for the record. It includes all texts read, with no editions credited for any. Also enclosed are four identical cards suitable for use in a library card catalogue. Multiple copies available of booklet, as stock number B9B 0994.

This elaborate set, carefully planned and packaged, features near-perfect pronunciation of the ME portion. A few errors do occur, especially during the fainting scene in Criseyde's bedroom: ModE vowels for "so" and "to," and an overlong vowel such that "ne" becomes "nay" (*Tr* 3.1086, 1089, 1116, 1136).

Dramatization, regrettably, occurs only about as often as mispronunciation. In *Troilus* isolated words and phrases sometimes project meanings, though without creating characters thereby. Pandarus sounds frightened as he utters "or we be lost," even while casting Troilus into bed in fulfillment of his plan, and sounds offended to be addressing a "thef" (*Tr* 3.1095, 1098). In the *General Prologue* the Wife of Bath's portrait conveys a progression of attitudes, all very mild, that could conceivably emit from one narrator.

At first he disapproves, especially of her anger in church (*GP* 451), but he comes to shrug benignly at her huge hat and to enjoy her knowledge of the remedies of love (*GP* 471-475). Elsewhere this latent narrator has no attitudes; the rest of the *General Prologue* is recited, not performed.

EAV, KE 90233B, cassette.
Chaucer's Canterbury Pilgrims. Middle English.
Reader Ronald A. Waldron.
1970.
Script editor Rhoda Gilinsky, project editor Anne S. Wax.
L. of C. #78-736862.
F. N. Robinson, *The Complete Works of Geoffrey Chaucer* (Boston: Houghton Mifflin, 1933).
Side 1, Introduction to *CT* as related to oral tradition; *GP* 1-8, 12-29, 43-50, 73-88, 93-96, 99-102, 109-10, 115-23, 137-41, 163-64a; *NPT* 3455-59; *GP* 165-68, 175-78, 189-92, 203-4, 208-11, 215-24, 235-40, 270-75, 279-96, 303-14, 323-24, 327-34, 339-46, 353-54, 357-60, 379-400, 411-22, 439-48, 456-62, 469-74, 477-82, 491-94, 515-16, 521-24, 545-46, 549-51, 562-75, 587-96, 613-16, 621-28, 634-38, 647-48, 666-70, 675-78, 693-95, 699-708, 715-24, 788-95, 769-70 (23 min., 36 sec.).
Side 2, The same lines keyed for automatic rather than manual projectors.
Enclosures: This cassette is one of two that accompany EAV's filmstrip B9KF 0233, with the same main title. The other cassette contains the same *GP* passages read in Modern English by Roy Skelton. Of the 29 frames on the filmstrip (made in 1963), 23 show the Ellesmere pilgrim portraits; also shown are the Gough map for

southeast England, a fifteenth-century map of Canterbury, and the portraits of Chaucer from Corpus Christi ms. 61 and Harleian ms. 4866. A ten-page Teacher's Notes, while crediting neither edition nor translation, provides a brief introduction and instructions for presentation, plus complete texts of the narration and both ModE and ME.

This reading of the *General Prologue* begins unpropitiously, from a gloomy narrator for whom spring forebodes trouble, but who perks up at the thought of nine and twenty new friends (*GP* 24). Occasionally he will return to his foreboding tone; usually, though, he is consistent in his recognition of pilgrims' shortcomings and in his reluctance to condemn any but the two worst of them, Reeve and Summoner. Though never particularly cheerful, he sometimes expresses mild amusement at such features as the Prioress's nasal singing, the pig bones displayed by the Pardoner, the Parson's pomposity, and the Clerk's emaciation—this last with a chuckle (*GP* 123, 700, 479, 288). He aims mild disapproval at the Pardoner's earnings and the Franklin's always-set table, and sterner disapproval at the Reeve's skinny legs and (gratuitously) at his horse Scot (*GP* 703-4, 353-54, 591, 615-16). The narrator sounds angry at the Reeve and angrier yet at the Summoner—in the latter case, however, also excited to be speaking from the very presence of the devil incarnate (especially on line 626).

Such attitudes are overt; the narrator conveys moral awareness in more subtle ways as well. In a hearty voice he imitates the Miller bragging about his own corn-stealing ability. But *we* know better, the narrator's tone assures on line 562. He conveys a double tone too in reference to the Monk's morality. The Monk himself claims in a hearty voice that the anti-hunting text is not worth a pulled hen; but we know better (*GP* 177-78). The narrator finds no moral problems in the Wife of Bath's behavior, however, checking his enthusiasm only to confide that her past is none of our business (*GP* 461-62). This better than adequate performance, although not a compelling one, is unified by the narrator's carefully expressed attitudes toward morally varying pilgrims. Consistency in pronunciation is more problematic. Most errors are the common ones: ModE cognates for many small words such as "he," "was," "so," and "ther," plus an occasional ModE long-*a* sound in lieu of schwa such that "bookes" seem "bookays" (*GP* 294). In an odder quirk, plurals twice emerge instead with a ModE long-*e* sound, such that the Merchant has "booties" and the Wife "hippies" (*GP* 273, 472). Inconsistency makes these errors hard to ignore. For example, the word "he" occurs nine times in the stretch *GP* 220-24, 235-40. The first three instances have ME vowels, the middle three ModE, the last three ME again.

EAV, KE 90395, cassette. No longer available as record, LE 5055.
Beowulf-Chaucer.
Readers John C. Pope for *Beowulf*, Helge Kökeritz for Chaucer.
1956.
L. of C. #R57-913/4.
F. N. Robinson, ed., *The Complete Works of Geoffrey Chaucer* (Boston: Houghton Mifflin, 1933).
Side 1, *Beowulf* 1-11, 26-53, 205-24a, 736b-70, 1159b-74, 1345-72, 2247-66, 3156-82 (11 min., 55 sec.).
Side 2, *GP* 1-42, 118-62, 285-308; *WBP* 453-80; *PriT* 516-50; *Tr* 1.1-35 (13:30).

Enclosure (with the tape): Eight-page booklet, of which six concern Pope's intentions in reading *Beowulf* as he does. Concerning Chaucer, a brief biography of Kökeritz refers readers to the complete phonetic transcriptions of the passages read, in his *Guide to Chaucer's Pronunciation* (1961; rpt. Toronto: U of Toronto P, in association with the Mediaeval Academy of America, 1978).

Because the author of *A Guide to Chaucer's Pronunciation*, generally regarded as definitive, herein reads the passages for which he has provided phonetic transcriptions, it is instructive to note the difficulty of recreating perfect ME pronunciation even by a widely acknowledged expert. While not frequent, his pronunciation errors do include the common ones of a final schwa that blends toward ModE long *a* (on "serve," *Tr* 1.15); an Anglicized *u* in "usage" (*PriT* 527); pronounced initial *h*s where the transcription urges silence (on "his," *GP* 295 and *PriT* 550, and "hir," *WBP* 461); and near-ModE vowels for "about," "to," and "so" (*GP* 158, *Tr* 1.13-14, 32).

Performance is perfunctory at best. Although the *General Prologue* narrator projects attitudes toward some pilgrims, he by no means becomes a unified character. He begins by disapproving of the Prioress, for example, but then wavers into light mockery (*GP* 118, 143). He reserves his strongest emotion for someone not even present, for he finds fat people extremely disgusting in comparison to the Clerk (*GP* 288).

In the *Wife of Bath's Prologue*, Chaucer's text provides abrupt mood changes, which here are followed again without creating a consistent speaker. When this Wife expounds on the relationship between wine and Venus, she whines like a spoiled child. Next she almost weeps at women's lack of defense (*WBP* 464-67). Line by line, throughout *WBP* 469-80, she keeps switching attitudes. She goes from a fondly smiling, senile old lady to a child peeved about her loss of beauty and pith; then she explodes into open anger for one line, trembles with defiance for a couplet, and closes with the mild determination of a storyteller returning from a tangent (*WBP* 479-80). One is left with an uneasy feeling that the text is performing the reader, not vice versa.

ENGLISH CLASSICS, XTV 17216-17, record.
Availability not checked.
The Nun's Priest's Tale (*Chaucer*).
Reader Kemp Malone.
Producer E. Chatain.
Side 1, *NPT* 2821-3186.
Side 2, *NPT* 3187-3462.

In this *Nun's Priest's Tale* the reader's boredom overwhelms and muffles almost completely the potential for dramatization in Chaucer's text. Conveyed by over-regularized meter, with vowels stretched to exaggerate strong stresses, ennui opens the Tale and recurs throughout for narrator and characters alike. For example, Pertelote's first exclamation is recited with exaggerated pitch shifts exactly like those of the narrator introducing it, at *NPT* 2888-91, and nothing differentiates between Chaunticleer's bored "solas" and the narrator's bored "cas" at *NPT* 3203-4.

When characterization does struggle to the surface, it is difficult to justify in terms of the text. Pertelote, after hearing about her husband's bad dream, explodes "Avoy!" in fury. She continues to threaten him viciously throughout *NPT*

2908-69. A long long pause ensues, during which Chaunticleer swallows his anger albeit not his pride. "Madame . . . graunt mercy of youre loore," he says slowly, but I am *very* very glad to present a list of authorities to the contrary, glad because I can thereby make you look like the fool that you are. After giving *exemplas* in this same self-satisfied tone, he proceeds without a break or tone shift to admire the beauty of her red face at *NPT* 3160. Perhaps he shares personality traits with the rooster who briskly offers a polite suggestion to the running fox beneath him, at *NPT* 3407-13, but the shared cool-headedness seem more coincidence than artistically intended characterization.

This performance's narrator seems an ill-tempered Nun's Priest indeed. He condemns everything and everybody, expressing (as examples) oppressive gloom toward the equally unappealing alternatives of free will and foreknowledge, bitter shame toward both Adam and "wommennes conseils," mockery toward Pertelote and her sisters sunbathing, and disdain toward the ladies of Ilion, Mrs. Hasdrubal, senators' wives, hens, and peasant women—all equally loud-mouthed and stupid (*NPT* 3234-51, 3256-58, 3267-69, 3355-3401). Nor does he spare the listeners to his sermon: "ye lordes" addresses direct scorn toward the idiots who will certainly continue to trust flattery despite hearing this Tale, at the end of which a supremely smug Nun's Priest gloats that only he, not his ignorant audience, knows its meaning (*NPT* 3325-30, 3436-43).

ModE vowels occur in "murier," "he," "tree," "bee," "was," "thise," "among his," " yow," and elsewhere (*NPT* 2851, 2876, 3139-40, 3189, 3201, 3313, 3410). It is definitely problems of performance not pronunciation, however, that mar this recording.

EVEREST, 3145/7, record in seven-unit series. Availability not checked. Apparently reissue of *English Medieval Christmas Carols*, Esoteric ES 521.

Noah Greenberg Conducting the New York Pro Musica: An Anthology of Their Greatest Works. Record 5: English Medieval Carols.
Performers Primavera Singers of New York Pro Musica.
1967? (orig. 1953).
Director Noah Greenberg.
Editions: John Stevens, ed., *Medieval Carols*, vol. 4 of *Musica Brittanica* (London: Stainer & Bell, 1952); Archibald T. Davison and Willi Apel, eds., *Historical Anthology of Music,* 2 vols. (Cambridge: Harvard UP, 1946).
Side 1, Latin song; Nowel sing we, Ave Maria, Lullay lullow, What tidings bringest thou messenger, Marvel not Joseph, Alma redemptoris mater.
Side 2, Latin songs; Make we joy now in this fest, Nowell nowell tidings true, Hail Mary full of grace, Ave rex angelorum, Nova nova.
Cover: Memorial tribute to Noah Greenberg.

EVERETT/EDWARDS, 3003, cassette.
The Canterbury Tales.
Lecturer Stephen Medcalf.
1973.
Side 1, Lecture which includes a few ME passages—*GP* 1-17, *WBP* 609-18, *KnT* 2456 ff., *ClT* 1142-55.
Special Note: Everett/Edwards also produces two other lectures by Medcalf, "Chaucer: The Art of Self Consciousness" (3001) and "Troilus and Criseyde" (3002). Probably each contains passages quoted in ME.

None are reviewed here because the format is outside the range of this discography.

EXPERIENCES ANONYMES, EA 0024, record in nine-unit series. Availability not checked. Apparently reissued as MHS 678.
Music of the Middle Ages. Vol. 4: English Polyphony of the 13th and Early 14th Centuries.
Performers Russell Oberlin, Charles Bressler, Donald Perry.
1957.
Producer Beverly Merrill, director Saville Clark.
Side 1, Latin songs; Worldes blis, Jesu Cristes milde moder.
Side 2, Latin songs; Foweles in the frith, Edi beo thu hevene quene.
Cover: Manuscript information and musicological considerations for each song by Denis Stevens.
Enclosure: Eight-page booklet with introduction, uncredited texts, glosses for ME, and translations for Latin.

EXPERIENCES ANONYMES, EA 0029, record in nine-unit series. Availability not checked.
Music of the Middle Ages. Vol. 5: English Medieval Songs [of the 12th and 13th Centuries].
Performer Russell Oberlin.
1957.
Producer Beverly Merrill.
Side 1, The St. Godric songs, Worldes blis ne last no throwe.
Side 2, Byrd one brere, Man mei longe him liues wene, Stond wel moder under rode.

Cover: Introduction to each song by Saville Clark.
Enclosure: Eight-page booklet with introduction and uncredited glossed texts.

FOLKWAYS, SC 9851, record.
Early English Poetry.
Reader Charles W. Dunn.
1958.
L. of C. #R59-65.
Charles W. Dunn, ed., *A Chaucer Reader* (New York: Harcourt Brace, 1952).
Side 1, band 1, Caedmon's Hymn.
    band 2, Battle of Maldon 273-319.
    band 3, Seafarer 1-64a.
    band 4, *Beowulf* 2724-2927, 2999-3057, 3076-3182.
Side 2, band 1, *Sir Gawain and the Green Knight* 2077-2211.
    band 2, *WBT* 857-1264.
Cover: Modern drawing of pastoral scene with ruins.
Enclosure: Twelve-page booklet with introduction to the record and to each work, plus all texts read. *Beowulf* is reproduced from F. Klaeber's edition (Heath, 1950) with C. W. Kennedy's translation (Oxford, 1940). The other Anglo-Saxon texts are reproduced from *Bright's Anglo-Saxon Reader* (Holt, 1953) with Dunn's own prose translations. For *SGGK* Dunn provides I. Gollancz's text (Oxford for E.E.T.S., 1940) and T. H. Banks's translation (Appleton-Century-Crofts, 1929). Glosses accompany Dunn's Chaucer text, along with a photograph and biography of Dunn.

This record contains a well-chosen selection of materials for courses in medieval literature or history of the language. Unfortunately, pronunciation and performance of the Chaucer portion are barely adequate. At far too many points to list, the ModE cognate is substituted for such common words as "many," "that," "have," "unto," "and," "but," and "now."

All characters sound bored. The two liveliest moments in the story are the eager relief of Midas's wife after telling the secret, and the final spat-out "pestilence" (*WBT* 977-78, 1264). This latter oath presumably conveys the attitude of the Wife of Bath, as does the self-conscious sarcasm with which she speaks of limitours replacing elves and incubi (*WBT* 873-81). As narrator, however, the Wife conveys no involvement with the plight of the old hag, whose lecture on "gentillesse" in particular seems an aural opiate intended to lull her groom to sleep. When she offers to fulfill his worldly appetites, a slight perking up of her tone rouses him (*WBT* 1218). Without the slightest conflict or hesitation, he hands the choice back to her and, presumably, curls back up with pillow over his head.

FOLKWAYS, FL 9858, record.
Lyrics from the Old English.
Reader Robert P. Creed.
1964.
ModE reader Burton Raffel.
Edition: G. P. Krapp and E. V. K. Dobbie (Columbia UP, 1931-53), adapted in accordance with work of Francis P. Magoun.

Caedmon's Hymn, Husband's Message, Ruin, Wulf and
Eadwacer, charm fragment, Genesis A 2846-2936
(Abraham and Isaac); riddles 1, 7, 8, 11, 29, 32;
Bede's Death Song.
Cover: Photograph of old house.
Enclosure: Twelve-page booklet with introduction to OE
poetry, stressing lyricism; texts and translations read;
credit for editions, other commentary, technical
assistance, and permission to print Raffel's ModE
translations from his *Poems from Old English* (U of
Nebraska P, 1964).

FOLKWAYS, FL 9859, record.
Chaucer. Readings from "Canterbury Tales."
Reader Victor L. Kaplan.
1962 (record), 1965 (booklet), 1966 (cover).
L. of C. #R62-1278.
Side 1 (FL 9859A), band 1, *GP* 1-41, 331-60, 477-520,
545-66, 715-24.
  band 2, *PardT* 661-888, 893-903.
Side 2 (FL 9859B), band 1, *NPT* 2984-3063.
  band 2, *NPT* 3215-3446.
  band 3, *Purse.*
  band 4, *Lak.*
Cover: Modern sketch of Chaucer (head and shoulders).
Enclosure: Twelve-page booklet, which contains a brief
introduction to Chaucer; guide to pronunciation;
biography of Kaplan; texts read and glosses. F. N.
Robinson is given credit for the text and Kaplan for the
glosses. Line numbering is provided as if each Tale
began at line one.

For these internally cohesive excerpts from the two most commonly anthologized Tales and the *General Prologue*, the oral interpretations—through not wide-ranging—are appropriate in each immediate context. For example, a self-satisfied tone, similar on personal pronouns in *GP* 31, 39, 359, and 492, in each case helps characterize. In lines 31 and 39 the pilgrim Chaucer is pleased at his ability to make friends more easily than he, a shy person, would have expected; line 359 conveys the Franklin's own self-satisfaction at election to political office, then, and line 492 the Parson's satisfaction at his own conscientiousness.

A similar self-satisfaction creeps into the voice of the old man in the *Pardoner's Tale*, as he points the riotours up the crooked way to the gruesome death trap they surely deserve for addressing him, a weak and senile whimperer, in brash scornful tones (*PardT* 715-67). Such scorn seems inappropriate, however, from the riotours who earlier asked the tavern boy about death with polite curiosity, and who set out on their honorable quest with a stirring vow (*PardT* 667-69, 692-701).

Characterization of the fox and chickens is more consistent, conveyed by a narrator who takes seriously the plight of such noble beasts (as conveyed by the apostrophes of *NPT* 3338-74). The two short poems sound appropriately teasing and glum, respectively, except that *Lak of Stedfastnesse* edges toward peevishness in the third stanza.

Pronunciation slips are slight and infrequent. For example, in *PardT* 671-72 the "houres" is correct, but the second syllable of its rhyme "youres" slides a bit too far from schwa toward a ModE long-*a* sound. In *PardT* 903, "unkynde" has a proper ME second vowel but a ModE "un."

GOLDEN CLARIOUN, 1RR, cassette.
The Romaunt of the Rose (Selections).
Readers Paul Piehler, George Bland.
1962.
Side 1, *Rom* 1-684, 729-58, 1455-68, 1543-1600 (43 min.).
Side 2, *Rom* 1601-1732, 1927-2032, 2135-2342, 2951-3337 (46 min.).
Cover: Contents.

In his youth Chaucer may have written the first 1705 lines of the 7696-line ME translation of *Romant de la Rose*. Rather appropriately, albeit without critical precedent or context, Golden Clarioun presents it as children's theater.

At the narrator's "Romance of the Rose!" (*Rom* 39), the curtain rises on a fairyland setting, which he continues to describe in skillfully varied tones until action begins. The narrator introduces in turn Hate, in a mean rusty voice that would do for the witch in *Hansel and Gretel*; Vilanye, as the evil queen in *Snow White*; and Coveitise, as a sort of Dickensian villainess (*Rom* 147-206). Not all allegorical figures threaten, though. Ydelnesse sounds languid and sensual, for instance, but not too languid to imitate the tra-la, tra-la with which Mirth is wont to enter the garden at *Rom* 615-17.

Within the probably non-Chaucerian portion a less skillful reader takes the role of Bialacoil, who turns tail and runs when a magnificently enacted hulk of a villain, Daunger, stomps onstage at line 3130. The Golden Clarioun narrator knows his audience well, and knows when and how to end the play. Cheers would greet the closing curtain as the narrator turns to Reason at line 3305 and says over and over, in different words but the same inflections time after time, inflections forbidden to children in the world off stage, "Oh shut *up*. Oh shut *up*. So *there*. Shut *up*." Given the length of the production and the rigidity of the material being nudged to life, Golden Clarioun can be forgiven relatively frequent errors in pronunciation, usually for pronouns and other cognates like "but." They jar only when a ME "be" follows hard on a ModE "he" in line 1593, for example, or when a garden with ModE long *e* in its second syllable occurs two lines before an accurate ME "gardyn" (*Rom* 481, 483).

GOLDEN CLARIOUN, 2BD, cassette.
The Book of the Duchess.
Reader Paul Piehler.
1971.
Albert C. Baugh, ed., *Chaucer's Major Poetry* (New York: Prentice-Hall, 1963).
Side 1, *BD* 1-709 (40 min.).
Side 2, *BD* 710-1334 (38 min.).
Cover: Contents.

Like the *Book of the Duchess* itself, this performance brings touches of humanity and characterization to a set of stiff literary conventions—but only touches. Juno commands as would a queen, for example, and Seys speaks like a ghost (*BD* 136-52, 201-11). Such opportunities are few. Were the narrator not already asleep, he might well become so during the Black Knight's interminably self-pitying description of his feelings about his lady before she succumbed. Subtypes of his self-pity include exhaustion (line 475 ff.), pouting (600 ff., 938 ff.), resentment (618 ff.), deathbed resignation (650 ff.), worshipful pathos (822 ff.), begging (866 ff.), and weepiness beginning about line 1198 and resulting at last in open tears for "She ys ded!" (*BD* 1309).

The narrator thereby accomplishes what he set out to do: to facilitate the Black Knight's grieving process by getting him to stop repressing his feelings. This psychologist/narrator is in control of situations throughout. At the opening, his own slight self-pity emerges only because he is very, very sleepy. Though surprised to see a man at all, he greets him heartily and tries to talk sports as men are wont to do (lines 448 ff., 522 ff., 539 ff.). Soon realizing that his new acquaintance, an intellectual, buries his feelings under massive citations of learning, the professional attains the patient's trust and respect with citations of his own (*BD* 725 ff.). Then, especially with lines 746-48, 1135-36, and 1139-43, he keeps urging that the Black Knight say outright what previously he had uttered only in private (i.e., in line 479). All in all, Golden Clarioun presents successfully, albeit not quite dynamically, one major critical interpretation of the poem.

Some pronunciation errors occur. They only occasionally intrude, as when a ModE "say" follows close on a ME "may," or when shut windows seem made of excrement (*BD* 705, 335). Except for the absence of "se" in line 913, the occasional textual changes do not affect sense (e.g., in *BD* 1065 "so have I" becomes "as I have").

GOLDEN CLARIOUN, 3HF(1) and 3HF(2), two cassettes
    available separately.
The House of Fame.
3HF(1):
Readers Paul Piehler, Kerrigan Prescott.

1963.
W. W. Skeat, ed., *The Works of Geoffrey Chaucer* (Oxford UP, 1894).
Side 1, *HF* 1-508 (26 min.).
Side 2, *HF* 509-1090 (26 min.).
Cover: Contents.

3HF(2):
Reader Paul Piehler.
1980.
Albert C. Baugh, ed., *Chaucer's Major Poetry* (New York: Prentice-Hall, 1963).
Side 1, *HF* 1091-1656 (25 min.).
Side 2, *HF* 1657-2156 (24 min.).
Cover: Contents.

Seventeen years passed between Golden Clarioun's taping of Books 1-2 and Book 3 of the work that supplies the company's name (in *HF* 1723). The 1980 reading, while correct and responsive to the text, sounds perfunctory compared to the energetic 1963 reading. In Books 1-2, the two readers fuse their parts so smoothly that, at first, one might think that a single reader is shifting to a deeper pitch for the eagle.

The fatherly eagle, like a very skilled junior-high-school science teacher, makes the lesson sound more and more exciting so that his student can imagine himself an adventure-show hero about to make a dramatic discovery about the nature of sound. In an endearing twist, then, at line 871 we hear that the eagle has been propounding a theory of his own, and genuinely wants a stranger's opinion on its validity. The performance amplifies the text's contrast between the dreamy philosopher Geffrey and this natural scientist trying to convince him to take his nose out of books and look around, particularly in the eagle's disappointment that his possible pupil does not care to learn star names even as adjunct to stories (*HF* 992 ff.).

Although his character is less fully realized than is the eagle's, the narrator Geffrey does make notably effective use of pauses. When asked how he fares, he utters an unsure "wel" only after long consideration (*HF* 888), and he listens carefully before terming the sound surflike in line 1034. Otherwise his attitudes are predictable: curious interest at first sight of the temple of glass, indignation at Juno's unfair treatment of Trojans and at men's abandonment of women, naive pride at counting himself among famous dreamers, and so on (*HF* 120 ff., 198 ff., 276 ff., 509 ff.).

Other characters also come to predictable life. Fame harshly commands those who seek fame, then sounds kind but firm to those who wish to hide their works (*HF* 1559-61, 1713-21). The groups are aurally distinguishable: those who want fame beg for it; those who want no fame ask with self-confident dignity; and those who have done nothing whatsoever sound quite like idle playboys (*HF* 1553-58, 1609-14, 1693-99, 1730-62).

The readings contain minor textual variants such as "hym of" for "of hym" in line 464. Pronunciation is extraordinarily accurate; in the entire performance occur only ModE "but"s in lines 119 and 140.

GOLDEN CLARIOUN, 5PF, cassette.
The Parlement of Foules.
Reader Paul Piehler.
1984.
Side 1, *PF* 1-637 (46 min.).
Side 2, *PF* 638-99 (5 min.).

Cover: Contents.

For Chaucer's most fully developed dream vision the Golden Clarioun narrator, only superficially Chaucer-the-naive-reader-and-dreamer, is certainly Chaucer-the-man, and very specifically Chaucer-the-birdwatcher. The catalogue of birds, which a cat-lover might find boring, projects the character of each bird described in quick line-by-line (or half-line) shifts. Like an aural slide show, lines 346-47 display in turn a scornful jay, a dangerous heron, a mean lapwing . . . and on to a haughty pheasant, a smirking greasy cormorant, a loud-mouthed know-it-all crow, and so on (*PF* 357, 362-63).

The three rival tercels have distinct personalities (*PF* 416-83). The first, the royal one, is accustomed to public speaking and accustomed to getting his own way, as long as he has followed proper forms of public conduct. The second tercel, of lower kind, talks faster. He accuses the first tercel rather than attempting to impress Nature or the lady. Probably he has never made a speech before. The third tercel knows how to make a public speech, but would prefer not to. His bursting heart drives him to make public his intensely private emotions, with reluctance conveyed particularly by sighs in lines 464 and 469. The three have their say before an impolite crowd (*PF* 492-97); a very polite, well-bred, self-contained formel; and a Dame Nature who is secretly on the formel's side all along, as is audible particularly in lines 409 and 627.

The tercels speak before a crowd made up of avian individuals. The terslet is sensible, for instance, and likes to set up situations in which he will shine: with a melodramatic pause before "batayle" in line 539, he knows that he will have eagle wings clutching for swords so that he, Terslet the Sensible, can step in to stop them. Characterization is particularly skillful in that the birds who speak twice do so with absolute consistency. The cuckoo seems a stage villain both times, evil for the sake of evil (*PF* 505-8, 605-9). Both times the goose speaks as an oaf, good-natured while trying to help figure things out, especially with his laboriously deduced last line (*PF* 501-4, 563-67). It is certainly a male goose's speech on Golden Clarioun despite the female pronoun in line 563. This gender-crossing oral interpretation casts a different light than usual on the poem, in which a female refuses all three male-defined choices. One comes to notice a sort of intermingling or questioning of male/female roles in the text—a questioning reinforced by the third bird with two speeches, the turtledove. She or he consistently speaks as a stereotyped male homosexual, with inflections particularly marked on "ded" in line 585.

A simple but effective aural detail ends the dream. The narrator vows to keep on reading books. An up-pitch on the work's final word "spare" reinforces the text with an orally projected "To Be Continued." The skillfully varied performance has contained no striking pronunciation errors, just occasional textual variants (e.g., one "ne" in line 439) and slips into ModE cognates of minor words (e.g., "of," "fyrst," "that," in *PF* 11, 35, 36, 62, 68, 70).

GOLDEN CLARIOUN. 6Tr(1) and 6Tr(2), two cassettes
    available separately.
Troilus and Criseyde (Selections).
6Tr(1):
Readers Paul Piehler, Kerrigan Prescott.
1963.
Albert C. Baugh, ed., *Chaucer's Major Poetry* (New York:
    Prentice-Hall, 1963).

Side 1, *Tr* 1.1-546 (38 min.).
Side 2, *Tr* 1.547-1064 (30 min.).
Cover: Contents.

6Tr(2):
Readers Paul Piehler, Kerrigan Prescott, Judy Lowder
    Newton, Maj-Britt Piehler.
1963 for Side 1, 1972 for Side 2.
Albert C. Baugh, ed., *Chaucer's Major Poetry* (New York:
    Prentice-Hall, 1963).
Side 1, *Tr* 2.85-595 (30 min.).
Side 2, *Tr* 3.1-49, 1114-1323; 4.1142-1246; 5.1786-1869
    (32 min.).
Cover: Contents.

Oddly, since plenty of tape time remains, 6Tr(1) stops four stanzas short of completing Book 1 of *Troilus*. The readers make a few minor pronunciation slips: for example, ModE cognates occasionally replace ME "to" (in 1.1 and 1.41), "answere" (1.69), and "may" (1.778). 6Tr(2) has lengthy, self-contained excerpts from Books 2 through 5; a reader announces each transition, usefully allowing time for page-flipping. Pronunciation errors are very infrequent—no *gh* in "nought" in *Tr* 2.146, for example—and no more intrusive than are the occasional textual variants, such as "why" for "what" in 2.223. One textual variant does matter, though: Criseyde utters no "ha ha" in 2.589. And among occasional microphone noises and other production flaws, one also matters: at 3.1202, a sound rather like crumpling aluminum foil occurs . . . just as Troilus first enfolds Criseyde in his arms!

Otherwise Golden Clarioun provides a fully satisfactory introduction to its speaking characters—Troilus, Pandarus, Criseyde—as well as a sense of the world around them. The

Trojan citizens express disgust at Calkas in 1.87, and the other young knights audibly share Troilus's brash adolescent swaggering in 1.183-89. Even Bayard draws us into the world of a high-born, pompous horse made suddenly sad at 1.223 by the demand for slave labor.

Although the text would allow for a whining, self-pitying protagonist, the Golden Clarioun Troilus maintains bemusement both toward love itself—a physical disease that makes him sound ill at times (e.g., 1.507 ff., 1.597 ff.)— and toward the idiosyncrasies of his best friend. He lets Pandarus indulge his fondness for long advisory speeches, with toleration particularly noticeable when Troilus agrees to hear all about Oënone at 1.657. In fact, he seems to express conventional "courtly-love" attitudes primarily to please or entertain Pandarus, who so enthusiastically wallows in the melodrama of his own broken heart (1.666-67).

Without Pandarus's immediate coaching, in the two bedroom scenes juxtaposed on this recording, Troilus is at a loss. In both interactions Criseyde take the lead, sounding soft and sexy when Troilus is bewildered (especially 3.1183 and 3.1309) and near-orgasmic with grief when he is baffled (4.1149-50). Not quite knowing what else to do at 4.1175-76, Troilus thinks of suicide, then sounds almost disappointed to have his decision thwarted at 4.1214-15. Criseyde is astonished, but secretly pleased that he would have killed himself for her sake (4.1231).

Strong though she be with her lover, Criseyde is no match for her uncle. When Pandarus first enters her house, intent on making her agree to love Troilus, she sounds pleased at his apparent interest in her reading (2.100-105). When he changes the subject to tease her about appropriately female activities, she is irritated but has no choice: she switches to the little-girl, flirtatious begging that he always wants to hear (2.131 ff.). Her fearfulness does not emerge until Pandarus forces it. She is first frightened at the intensity with which he peers at her (2.276-77), and more so when he replies in a vicious tone fully intended to scare her. By 2.309-14 she is squeaky with panic. A slow and sinister Pandarus threatens to cut his throat in tones that might well cause her to fear implications for her own throat (2.325). Confronting such a monstrous em, she sounds scared even in her private thought, 2.387, which some critics consider cunning. A slight defiance in her tone at "blisful cas" (2.422) evokes from Pandarus an even angrier reply.

Weeping, left with no alternatives, this Criseyde reluctantly but determinedly makes up her mind. Her voice firms up noticeably through her vow (2.484-89), and by 2.499-504 she decides to return to the little-girl-curious role that she knows will sooth her uncle's seething temper. Indeed Pandarus, promptly pacified, delivers in kind tones his lie about Troilus in the garden (2.506 ff.).

Seeing Pandarus so in control, both of textual action and characters' reactions to each other, the Golden Clarioun narrator relinquishes power to him as well. Never fully characterized, this narrator opens Book 1 in a sepulchral, doom-laden voice to which he sometimes reverts (e.g., at 1.302-7). He closes Book 5 with attitudes that lurch back and forth without quite meshing. Though sad that pagan rites are no more and none too enthusiastic about rejecting the world (5.1849-55, 5.1816-19), he is ready to laugh along with Troilus at the world's folly, and he delivers a sincere, kindly lecture to young folks about Christian values (5.1821-25, 1835-48). Whether Christian or pagan, at any rate, with a sigh at 5.1799 he wishes that he could avoid telling how Troilus finally died. He is tired, it seems, of telling stories.

GOLDEN CLARIOUN, 10GP, cassette.
General Prologue.
Readers Paul Piehler, Maj-britt Piehler.
1972.
Albert C. Baugh, ed., *Chaucer's Major Poetry* (New York: Prentice-Hall, 1963).
Side 1, *GP* 1-444 (28 min.).
Side 2, *GP* 445-858 (26 min.).
Cover: Contents.

Except for the Prioress's portrait to be discussed, the first one-third of this recording ranks with the best *General Prologue*s available. The self-confident narrator sets out at a brisk pace, effortlessly and enthusiastically introducing characters whose devoutness, like his own in line 22, is somewhat perfunctory.

Until the Clerk, this narrator consistently steps aside to hold the spotlight while each pilgrim tells us a little bit about himself. The Knight is a patriotic hero, a John Wayne for England, especially as he lists the abstractions on account of which he is protecting your freedom and mine (*GP* 45-46). His son loves to admire himself in the mirror (*GP* 80-84). The Yeoman, the Monk, and the Friar are likewise consistent in their enthusiasm for their own activities and attitudes.

Something strange happens at the Clerk's portrait, though, something so marked that it seems almost to have happened because of the Clerk. It could be the Clerk's own secretive voice describing himself throughout *GP* 285-308, especially in that lines 304-5 loudly imitate his occasional, but always profound, virtuous high speeches. After this point, though, all pilgrims retreat into one of the Clerk's books. Each is described by a kindly narrator confiding, in uniformly secretive tones, how that pilgrim behaves. The occasional deviations characterize the narrator, not the pilgrim as in the first third. He sounds tongue-in-cheek about the Lawyer's apparent busyness in *GP* 322, for example, and with a pause before "pigges" in line 700 seems to be teasing someone about the Pardoner's relics.

It is a shame that such a promising performance collapses so inexplicably, especially since pronunciation is near-perfect. Only seven ModE cognates occur, all minor: "mayde," "symple," "by," "he," "of," "ye," and "be" (*GP* 69, 319, 570, 609, 628, 780, 854). As an artistic whole the performance was already disrupted, unfortunately, in that a woman recites, rather than enacts, the Prioress's portrait (only). Although in theory this feature might accord with portraits enacted as if by each pilgrim, in practice it breaks the frame irreparably.

GOLDEN CLARIOUN, 10 GPB, cassette.
General Prologue for Beginners.
Reader Paul Piehler.
1986.
Side 1, *GP* 1-566 (48 min.).
Side 2, *GP* 567-858 (27 min.).
Cover: Contents.

In this *General Prologue* read very slowly, long pauses within and between lines nearly always separate sense units. (An exception would be "whan the . . . sonne" in *GP* 30.) Charmingly, even the ModE introductions are read very slowly: "This is . . . side two . . . of the Golden . . . Clarioun . . . recording of. . . ."

The pauses at first make the narrator seem a hesitant character. Gradually his opinions, sometimes strong ones, emerge. The Merchant is definitely suspect, for example: an "uh" before "sooth" in *GP* 284 makes clear that he intentionally conceals his name. On the other hand, this narrator retains the oft-noted ambiguity that ends the Prioress's portrait: an up-pitch at the end of line 162 adds a vocal question mark to the brooch's motto, "Love conquers all?"

Although certainly a lively reading, especially considering its speed, aesthetically this performance wavers back and forth between the narrator's attitude toward each pilgrim and that pilgrim's attitude toward himself. The Monk and Friar can serve as examples. The two portraits come complete with sound effects: a resonantly sung "In principio" in *GP* 254, and orally created onomatopoeia such that lines 169-71 imitate mellow bells jingling in the gentle breeze of the Monk's horse's slow pace. By means of pauses before "old" and "somdel" in line 174, then, the narrator signals to listeners that oldness and streitness are no excuses for breaking monastery rules; similarly, his pause before "fair" in line 204 signals that a Monk's physical appearance ought not to elicit praise. In the rest of the portrait, instead, the Monk gives his own opinion of his complexion, just as earlier he tells what he thinks about oysterlike texts and (with an openly scornful laugh on line 181) homebound monks.

For the Friar the proportions are reversed. He expresses his opinion of himself just in lines 246-61. Elsewhere the narrator calls into question the Friar's behavior by means of vocally created question marks (e.g., an up-pitch on "wommen" in *GP* 213), pauses (e.g., before "worthy" in *GP* 243), chuckles (e.g., *GP* 232), and tones of disapproval (e.g., *GP* 240).

Similarly split attitudes can be heard for most other portraits. However, this relatively sophisticated aesthetic problem would not interfere with use of the tape for its primary purpose, beginning students' comprehension of the language itself. Pronunciation falls short of perfection due to occasional ModE cognates for minor words such as "he," "his," "that," and "but" (e.g., *GP* 74, 76, 102, 518), and for "ynogh" in line 373 and "first" in line 725.

GOLDEN CLARIOUN, 11 KnT, cassette.
The Knight's Tale.
Reader Paul Piehler.
1972.
Albert C. Baugh, ed., *Chaucer's Major Poetry* (New York: Prentice-Hall, 1963).
Side 1, *KnT* 859-1186, 1696-1869 (30 min.).
Side 2, *KnT* 1918-2088, 2438-2478, 2595-2635, 2853-3108 (33 min.).
Cover: Contents.

Golden Clarioun has carefully chosen passages of the *Knight's Tale* suitable for listeners with about an hour to spend in class or language lab. In between the excerpts, each one internally coherent, the reader announces the next set of line numbers and, while listeners are finding the place in their texts, gives a brief summary of what is being skipped and/or what they are about to hear.

Duke Theseus is a pleasant and conscientious monarch. He commands the weeping widows with tones of concern in *KnT* 905-11, and sounds genuinely troubled by pointless bloodshed when he stops the fight in the grove (*KnT* 1706-13). His harshest anger he aims at himself, in lines 1773-81, irritated at having lost his temper.

Characters other than Theseus are less complex, indeed bland. Palamon's first "A!" is a loud grunt, such that the sight of Emelye seems to kick him hard in the stomach. Arcite responds with concern echoing Theseus's, then announces his own love (*KnT* 1079-91, 1118-22). Palamon pouts; Arcite pouts; Palamon speeds up in indignation; Arcite replies in spite, which he succeeds then in transferring from their rivalry to their common imprisonment, thus seeming slightly more mature than his cousin (*KnT* 1125-86).

The narrator starts out with plenty of variety, his tones responsive to both the story's action and the storytelling context, as in the friendly chattiness of line 1000. By the end he is flagging, though. Tournament action in lines 2595-2651 sounds no faster or more exciting than do actions in preparation for the funeral in 2853-2986. The tournament seems outright tedious, in fact, partly because of emphasis on third-person pronouns: *he* did this, *he* did that, *he* did the other, *he* did the same but from a slightly different angle, and on and on. In the last few lines the narrator does brighten his voice for the wedding festivities on *KnT* 3097-98, and he prays devoutly to God.

Saturn speaks with quiet dignity in lines 2453-78. The widows speak with quiet dignity in lines 915-47. The widows differ from Palamon in that they "knelen" with *k* pronounced, whereas Palamon falls on his knees with a ME vowel but no *k* (*KnT* 897, 1103). Two sisters and a queen elicit ModE vowels in lines 971, 1820, and 3075. Pronunciation seldom slips otherwise. The phrase "depeynted was" is reversed in line 2049; and the reader, as might any medieval scribe, substitutes "better" for "gretter," "has" for "hath," and "was" for "were" in *KnT* 1165, 1974, and 2596.

GOLDEN CLARIOUN, 12MiT, cassette.
The Miller's Tale.
Reader Paul Piehler.
1986.
Side 1, *MlrT* 3109-3521 (30 min.).
Side 2, *MlrT* 3522-3854 (22 min.).
Cover: Contents.

Imagine a *Miller's Tale* told by an ill-tempered misanthrope whose joyless lechery casts a pall over all activities among young people whom he resents. Imagine a *Miller's Tale* in which the liveliest speech is by Gerveys, who teases Absolon heartily, then expresses genuine curiosity (*MlrT* 3767-71, 3779-82). Imagine a shot-window scene related by a narrator offended that a woman has no beard, a scene in which Alisoun scolds lines 3728-29 and utters only one syllable of that great Chaucerian word "tehee," to which Absolon responds with viciously resentful disgust and receives in return a viciously resentful "fart" in line 3806. Imagine a narrator aware throughout that "queynte" is a disgusting word (especially *MlrT* 3605, 3754), but who nonetheless ignores the pun in lines 3275-76 in favor of a tone of grim foreboding. While grabbing Alisoun by the haunchbones and other places, Nicholas whispers urgently of horrors in the next passageway. Then he whines lines 3280-81. Alisoun echoes him, urgently whispering line 3284 and whining 3285-87. Flattered, perhaps, Nicholas metamorphoses into a kindly father figure to reassure her in lines 3298-3300.

Given the high artistic quality of most Golden Clarioun performances, one must regret the decision to release a recording in which orally expressed moods and attitudes relate only arbitrarily to the words of the text being correctly pronounced. Occasional lapses do occur to ModE cognates, mostly for pronouns and conjunctions except for a ModE "bird" replacing "bryd" in line 3699 (but not in 3805). A "hir" replacing "his" in line 3692 marks Absolon's questionable sexuality or singularity.

GOLDEN CLARIOUN, 13 ReT, cassette.
The Reeve's Tale.
Reader Paul Piehler.
1975.
Side 1, *RvT* 3855-4424 (32 min.).
Side 2, Blank.
Cover: Contents.

What a nasty little story this becomes with all traces of humor repressed. Only at line 4306, when the miller's wife baps his glinting skull, does slight amusement edge momentarily into this narrator's voice. Elsewhere he resents everything that many readers find funny. He resents the wife's airs, and resents the onomatopoetic "yexeth" and other features of the Symkyns' concert of snores and related bodily sounds (*RvT* 3942 ff., 4149 ff.). Perhaps such bitterness is meant to characterize the pilgrim Reeve as narrator. He sounds more tired than resentful, though, when he addresses the throng directly in *RvT* 3909 ff.

Resentment dominates all characters' speeches within the Tale as well as the narration. Even the horse sounds sinister in line 4066. Apparently it chases wild mares with the same asexual joylessness that drives the clerks to their night's revenge—Aleyn in spite at Symkyn, and John in spite at Aleyn (*RvT* 4169-4210). The narrator reinforces the lustlessness by snarling about John's hard, deep, mad pricking (*RvT* 4230-31). Aleyn rapes Malyne with less overt hostility, even though he does hustle from bed paying no mind whatsoever to her tears. He then brags about his consummate skill at degradation and insult (*RvT* 4247-67). In sum, no one gets excited anywhere in the Tale—not at sex nor escaped horses nor clerks tussling in one's bedchamber. The only pronunciation problems are ModE cognates for "herte," "dotage," and "derk" (*RvT* 3870, 3898, 4225).

GOLDEN CLARIOUN, 16 WBP, cassette.
The Wife of Bath's Prologue.
Reader Paul Piehler.
1980.
Albert C. Baugh, ed., *Chaucer's Major Poetry* (New York: Prentice-Hall, 1963).
Side 1, *WBP* 1-452 (32 min.).
Side 2, *WBP* 453-856 (29 min.).
Cover: Contents.

This recording of the Wife's oral autobiography, with adequate if not gripping characterization and only a few pronunciation slips (e.g., "noght" in *WBP* 159 and "gnat" in 347 both lack *g*s), might prove distracting for students unused to Middle English, on account of the numerous word substitutions, eliminations, additions, and inversions. At least twenty-nine orally created variants affect 3% of the lines of the *Prologue*. Most do not interfere with sense: an added "in" before "body," "yeven me" for "me yeven," and so on (*WBP* 97, 212). Also, changes even involving several syllables demonstrably do not interfere with smooth aural meter, despite editorial theories and worries to the contrary. *WBP* 368 flows fine without "maner," for example.

In the Golden Clarioun characterization, the many-faceted Wife openly delights in her arguments against scripture, chuckling on lines 20 and 36, and after 71 pausing before she crows with joy her clincher. Her references to virginity project self-conscious awareness that she has set up a false dichotomy, virginity vs. multiple marriages, with no middle. In line 105, for example, she makes virginity sound like a crashing bore.

Certainly no husband of hers would ever be bored. She keeps husbands spinning with line-by-line tone shifts: pouting in line 238, indignation next, and so on. It is social/marital interaction that enlivens her, though. Left to her own thoughts of past youth in *WBP* 469-79, she fades from liquor-induced heartiness to sadness, with a big sigh before line 472 and a distinctly mirthless 479. After a long pause, she converts her resentment about old age to resentment about her fourth husband, recalling gleefully in line 494 how she tortured him. Her fifth husband's reciprocal torture she accepts with a sigh, in line 505. She goes on to speak of Jankyn as if of someone else's spoiled child, making clear that his book describes some but by no means all women (e.g., with louder "hir"s in *WBP* 736), and laughing as he falls toward the flames.

The response to her Prologue features a jolly Summoner who teases, a bit too pointedly, a Friar who is surprised at the attack but promptly produces a good idea for the tale-telling contest (*WBP* 830-43). The Wife then flirts, of course; it is close to impossible to read aloud *WBP* 854-55 without fluttering one's eyelashes.

GOLDEN CLARIOUN, 16WBT, cassette.
The Wife of Bath's Tale.

Reader Paul Piehler.
1986.
Side 1, *WBT* 857-1264 (33 min.).
Side 2, Blank.
Cover: Contents.

The personality of the Golden Clarioun Wife of Bath has barely peeked through her choice of Tale, one realizes when she herself returns after a long pause midway in *WBT* 1258. Perhaps she also chuckles at the success of the old hag's trick, in *WBT* 1072. Otherwise, the story is told by a semi-professional storyteller who puts plenty of vocal variety into the Midas story, for example, or into the account of the search (*WBT* 919-82) wherein orally created onomatopoeia enlivens the replies, "jolynesse" sounding jolly and "lust" lustful. Furthermore, line 967 swells, 971 flames, and so on.

The two main characters are dramatized, though not with full artistic consistency. The knight has long since accepted his ensuing death when he addresses the hag as if she is his literal, concerned mother (*WBT* 1005-8). No potential for acceptance of his marital situation, in contrast, appears in his rude address to her a hundred lines later. The insulting inflections of "nay, nay!" (*WBT* 1098) imply that even a hideously ugly poor old man would reject her. He thus affronts the aging coquette who speaks lines 1087-97; by 1112 she has scrubbed off the thick make-up, and donned schoolmarm's spectacles to scold him roundly. Neither of these two attitudes quite coincides with the hag's first appearance, as an otherworldly creature guarding her grove and her secret (*WBT* 1001-4, 1009-12).

Whoever she is, marriage brings to the hag and the knight a lifetime of calm companionship, not of passion (*WBT* 1255-1258a). Almost no pronunciation errors mar that potential for peacefulness—just ModE cognates for "thynges," "answere" (followed by a ME "answerde" six lines later), and "to" and "fro" (*WBT* 876, 1029, 1085).

GOLDEN CLARIOUN, 17FrT, cassette.
The Friar's Tale.
Reader Paul Piehler.
1980.
Side 1, *FriT* 1265-1664 (28 min.).
Side 2, Blank.
Cover: Contents.

Like its companion Golden Clarioun *Summoner's Tale* (18*SuT*), this *Friar's Tale* aims its barb straight at the person present who shares its protagonist's profession, using a technique found in real-life storytelling sessions now and, insofar as can be determined, in the Middle Ages. This Golden Clarioun Friar tries to prod the Summoner to anger, yet loses the oral contest. Nonchalance is essential, in the unstated rules outlined by Carl Lindahl in his *Earnest Games: Folkloric Patterns in The Canterbury Tales*. One must pretend to be simply telling a story, not slurring one's opponent. The text's Miller wins over the Reeve, for example: compare *MlrT* 3151-66 to the Reeve's incompetently direct attack, *RvT* 3909-20 and 4324. Although Chaucer's text leaves the Friar/Summoner battle unresolved, Golden Clarioun resolves it in performance especially in *FriT* 1279, with pauses before and after "somonour," and in the very last line 1664, in which a pause followed by loud "hem" makes clear that the term "somonours" includes or indeed consists of present company.

In this final couplet, the Golden Clarioun Friar offers to the pilgrim Summoner the chance for repentance rejected by his Tale's summoner (*FriT* 1630-33). He thereby seems more tolerant than the Golden Clarioun Summoner, who makes a total cipher of his Tale's friar (cf. 18SuT). This Friar is less intent on oral character denigration than is his adversary, too, for the summoner in the Golden Clarioun *Friar's Tale* seems a pleasant enough fellow who confides naively in his new acquaintance, sounding jolly and eager to share the fun (*FriT* 1434-44). Upon learning the fiend's identity, he expresses genuine scientific curiosity. Within this performance he shares his relatively pleasant personality with the pilgrim Summoner, who at *FriT* 1332-33 interrupts the Friar to point out an inaccurate detail in the accusation.

The Tales of Friar and Summoner are seldom anthologized because of obscenity and inextricability from context. The advanced students likely to use this tape would not, therefore, be confused by textual variants such as "was" for "nas," "summon" for "sompne," a missing "eek," or an added "thee" (*FriT* 1322, 1577, 1295, 1527), nor by occasional slips such as a ModE "answer" (1596).

GOLDEN CLARIOUN, 18SuT, cassette.
The Summoner's Tale.
Reader Paul Piehler.
1986.
Side 1, *SumT* 1665-2294 (45 min.).
Side 2, Blank.
Cover: Contents.

On Golden Clarioun, the pilgrim Friar loses and the Summoner wins this round (cf. Golden Clarioun 17FrT).

Despite all the anger specified in the text of Summoner's Prologue and Tale both, the harshest anger here emerges from the Host as he shushes the pouty Friar and eagerly encourages the Summoner at *SumT* 1762-63. To remain calm throughout, the Golden Clarioun Summoner must ignore his opening stage direction, for he does not quake with ire at *SumT* 1667. He does curse the Friar with line 1707, though.

The friar in the Tale fools no one. Thomas, Thomas's wife, lord, lord's wife, Jankyn—all know him and his ways all too well. He greets Thomas with a spooky tone: time to administer extreme unction (*SumT* 1770-74, 1784-97). Thomas sounds friendly, not sick despite these efforts, but considers his wife's whereabouts none of the friar's business (*SumT* 1781-83, 1798-99). She tolerates the oily flirtatiousness with a sigh in line 1811, and perhaps a wink to her husband, "Oh, don't worry, he always acts this way until fed and sent along." Although nobody sounds angry, the friar passes the time until dinner with a generic, oft-rehearsed sermon on Anger. Thomas, waking from a doze at line 2094, replies with strained patience. In *SumT* 2124-26 and 2140-43 his voice remains under control so as to fool the increasingly petulant beggar. Petulance shifts to pouty prissiness after the friar receives the gift. He retains this tone to address the lord, who is quite as accustomed as is Thomas's wife to dealing with this fussbudget (*SumT* 2153-55, 2170-75).

When not even the lord's wife takes him seriously, in *SumT* 2205-9, the friar at last expresses open anger. The lord ignores him in *SumT* 2218 ff.; a mere page imitates the friar's poutiness in 2275-77, then mocks him; the pilgrim Summoner allows him only a pointedly parenthesized aside in line 2287. The Summoner has annihilated his opponent by means of a Tale which contains only a few pronunciation problems (e.g., ModE "we" and "be" in *SumT* 1794, 1807, 1879, 2249) and unobtrusive word substitutions including "my" for "his" and "upon" for "by" (*SumT* 1868, 2137).

GOLDEN CLARIOUN, 19ClT, cassette.
The Clerk's Tale.
Reader Paul Piehler.
1980.
Side 1, *ClT* 1-686 (47 min.).
Side 2, *ClT* 687-1212 (36 min.).
Cover: Contents.

In line 14 of the Prologue to the *Clerk's Tale*, the Host begs "that thy tale make us nat to slepe." Perhaps, then, it is characterization of a Clerk unable to comply with his behest which keeps this performance so dreary. A slow, pompous narrator becomes more so at any philosophical issue, such as death's imminence in *ClT* 36-38. Monotony makes an unpleasant story almost unbearably so. For example, the performance shows that, by choosing Grisilde so abruptly while wedding coach and rich array loom behind, Walter not only denies her the anticipation of a happy future life but also denies her free choice in stating her amazed vow of unthinking obedience at lines 344-64.

Janicula's pre-wedding speeches, like his daughter's, convey stupified amazement or, in her case, just plain stupidity. This Grisilde never learns much. She responds to Walter's accusation of unpopularity (*ClT* 477-90) with no awareness whatsoever that the people's action in lines 425-41 contradict his words, for example; and she addresses her returned children in 1088-98 as if she has spent eight years laboriously memorizing one simple fact about missing children. Walter's marriage to someone who, with training, has managed to learn how to obey his tones of self-satisfied pomposity, does make a certain kind of sense of the Tale. Although most pronunciation is correct, the first vowel of "herte" and the last syllable of "ynogh" always sound like their ModE equivalents, and occasional other slips occur (e.g., ModE "but" in *ClT* 206 and 211).

GOLDEN CLARIOUN, 20MeT, cassette.
The Merchant's Tale.
Reader Paul Piehler.
1980.
Side 1, *McIT* 1213-1874 (43 min.).
Side 2, *McIT* 1875-2440 (38 min.).
Cover: Contents.

Does the Merchant tell a bleak Tale because of bitterness about his own marriage, or does he joke about his new wife and proceed to a funny fabliau? Critics' extensive arguments about the Merchant's tone of voice stem in part from quotation marks, which were first added to a *Canterbury Tales* edition in 1847. Reproducing Thomas Wright's punctuation, editors since then have likewise assigned *McIT* 1267-1392, the encomium on marriage, to the Merchant rather than to January. Thus, readers since 1847 have had to imagine the Merchant spouting unabated sarcasm for 125 lines.

In the Golden Clarioun reading of this passage, the narrator maintains a bitterly sarcastic tone for only about ten lines. After line 1276 the oral praise gradually becomes what it would be on paper, if quotation marks set apart lines 1267-1392. It becomes the speech of January, here as elsewhere in the Tale uttering lecherous, self-satisfied delight overlaid with an overwhelmingly open-mouthed dullness. The oral characterization is particularly skillful in *MctT* 2069-96, wherein the narrator imitates January's mood shifts at the onset of blindness. He sobs mindless sympathy in lines 2069-71, stupidly wails 2072, flames with dull-witted jealousy in 2073, brightens stupidly for 2081, re-darkens his doltish mood in 2085-86, and so on.

At most points, though, the narrator has little sympathy for January but quite a lot for Damyan. This oral interpretation accentuates details of Chaucer's artistry in creating this work for oral delivery. For example, by giving lines 1869-74 to a potentially sympathetic narrator rather than to Damyan, Chaucer has freed the reader-aloud from any compulsion to whine "courtly-love" sentiments. Otherwise the narrator tells the story without drawing much attention to his own personality, not even for his oft-noted apologies (*McTT* 1951, 2350-51, 2362-63).

In the closing scene of adultery in the pear tree, a listener's sympathy might shift to January despite the narrator. While undergoing cuckoldry the foolish old man sounds weak, helpless, in his second childhood. His first exclamation, for example, is senile and pathetic; his question in line 2367 expresses bewilderment, not accusation or other possibilities. The Golden Clarioun May has had the deck stacked for her, by Proserpyne, and wins effortlessly over a distinctly unformidable opponent.

As to technicalities, a microphone problem interferes with line 1820. ModE vowels occasionally creep into cognates including pronouns and "semed," "usage," "tayl," and "used" (*McTT* 1743, 1861, 2060, 2149). Only two jar a bit: in 2165 the "I" has the value of a ModE long *a*; and in 1835-37, each containing the word "we," a reverse Great

Vowel Shift takes place, step by step from a ModE "we" to a ME one.

GOLDEN CLARIOUN, 22 FkT, cassette.
The Franklin's Tale.
Reader Paul Piehler.
1986.
Side 1, *FrkT* 673-1260 (48 min.).
Side 2, *FrkT* 1261-1624 (30 min.).
Cover: Contents.

Why have so few recordings been made of a Tale so well loved as the Franklin's? This performance suggests why: the text makes almost unavoidable a continual tone of whining, inaudible on the page but quite maddening aloud.

Aurelius's brother does not whine. Neither does the clerk, who comes to sound more and more like a cartoon-show Merlin the Magician (especially in *FrkT* 1587-91). Aurelius, however, stops whining only one time, to express fear in 967-71. Dorigen stops whining only to express fear of her husband (*FrkT* 754-59), indignation at God and at Aurelius (*FrkT* 875-84, 980-87), and staring-eyed madness for line 1512 only (she whines 1513). Unlike the lusty men who whine "Nowel" in *FrkT* 1255, Arveragus expresses other moods before heroically repressing (especially with a sniff after 1486) the tears specified. With line 1469 he suspects that Dorigen and the squire have done more than she said. Then he maintains a commanding nonchalance until line 1480 demands that he add to the salt flood.

The Franklin weeps but once, fortunately (*FrkT* 894). He sounds most happy while finishing the Tale, delighted at the conversation his question will initiate, and sounds least happy while interjecting a conventional moral into *FrkT* 1541-44. His personality emerges also in interaction with the Host, as he expresses amazement at the latter's vehement rudeness (*FrkT* 695-701), and in implied interaction with the Wife of Bath, as he tiptoes carefully past mention of wives in lines 743 and 818. His voice helps along the story by heartily bringing Arveragus home in *FrkT* 1087 ff., for example, and by wondering at the disappearance of the revel in line 1204. Overall, though, this Franklin would do better to keep serving good meals that attract master storytellers, instead of trying to sustain after-dinner entertainment on his own.

More pronunciation errors occur than are usual on Golden Clarioun recordings. "Herte" and its rhyme words, such as "asterte" in *FrkT* 1021-22, always have the ModE vowel. The pronoun "hir" sometimes becomes its ModE cognate—e.g., a ModE "her" in line 790 is followed by two ME "hir"s in 792. "Caught" in line 740 and "sighte" in 1058 have both lost their *g*s, and a "himselven" for "hirselven" changes the story of Habradate in 1415.

GOLDEN CLARIOUN, 24 PdT, cassette.
The Pardoner's Tale.
Reader Paul Piehler.
1972.
Albert C. Baugh, ed., *Chaucer's Major Poetry* (New York: Prentice-Hall, 1963).
Side 1, *PardT* 287-660 (21 min.).
Side 2, *PardT* 661-968 (18 min.).
Cover: Contents.

Unfortunately, this artistically fine performance is marred by production flaws. Too often to ignore, clicks are audible as the reader switches off the mike, then returns sometimes having skipped words. On this tape line 389 begins with the word "gaude" and 750 with "olde," for example. Most distractingly, the middle is missing from the much-discussed transition line 915, here as "As ye were . . . sires, thus I preche."

The Golden Clarioun Pardoner starts out by confiding in the pilgrims, chuckling at the gullible, and showing off by rattling *PardT* 341-45 without a pause. By line 359 the pilgrim audience has begun to fade. Excepting only line 555, an amused aside to the logical, the Pardoner delivers his entire sermon with the full-throated, guilt-inducing excitement long proven effective toward unbuckling of purses. Beginning at line 463, after confiding to the pilgrims that drinking and wenching can be just as sinister as cheating widows (*PardT* 450-53), this professional orator gasps his horror at the sins described. He whispers of danger in line 484, then almost shouts indignation at Lot and Herod. With skillfully varied tones, he does lines 517-19 in relaxing rocking rhythm before a return to indignation, followed by 530-35a as the voice of a prophet crying in the wilderness. Midpoint in line 535 he switches abruptly to weepiness, and practically produces tears before controlling himself, with a gulp, in 547-48. And so on, with never a dull moment.

Contrasts among Tale characters' vocal tones are there, certainly, though not so strikingly effective as all these contrasts within the Pardoner's own injunctions. The Golden Clarioun riotours are teenagers who have drunk a bit more than they can handle. They meet an unperturbed old man who lectures them briefly on acceptable adolescent behavior (*PardT* 739-49). They start to reply calmly but then YELL the first half of line 755 and beyond. Listeners may jump; the old man remains cool. Only one of the riotours seems evil enough to deserve their gruesome death. With a pause midway in line 785, this one is already thinking how to kill not only the youngest but also the duller-witted comrade to whom he will carefully explain, with pauses, how "us . . . thre" can become "us . . . two" (*PardT* 812, 814).

After the tape gap at line 915, the Pardoner seems to join one troop of Pardoners described by Chaucer critics—those Pardoners who, surprised at seeing the pilgrims caught up in the rhetoric, sincerely try to sell them pardons. He maintains a used-car salesman's tone of camaraderie—"Hey hey hey! Have I got a deal for you!"—and adds authenticity with a church-Latin chant for lines 939-40. The Host is amazed to be addressed. He starts sounding angry but by line 950, perhaps amused at the creativity of his own insults, ends nearly chuckling. All interactions are very accurately pronounced; throughout, ModE cognates occur only for "reed" and "botelles," *PardT* 744 and 871.

GOLDEN CLARIOUN, 26PrT, 27TST, one cassette with both stock numbers.
The Prioress's Tale and the Tale of Sir Thopas.
Reader Paul Piehler.
1986.
Side 1, *ShipT* 435-52, *PriT* 453-690, *Thop* 691-966 (36 min.).
Side 2, Blank.
Cover: Contents.

Because of anti-Semitism in the *Prioress's Tale* and sophisticated parody in *Thopas*, the two are seldom anthologized. The advanced students likely to use this tape would be treated to a remarkable dramatization of the interaction of the Host, Prioress, and Chaucer-the-naive-pilgrim as performed by Chaucer-the-genial-author. The very sparse pronunciation errors, such as ModE "felawe" in *PriT* 530, pass unnoticed in the heat of performance.

The Golden Clarioun Host shows respect toward clergy, using breathy pauses to address the Prioress and overtones of church-Latin chant to deem good, prematurely, Chaucer's choice of rhyme (*ShipT* 447-51, *Thop* 710-11). Although jolly, laughing aloud at *ShipT* 439, he takes responsibility seriously. Deeply upset that Chaucer's "rym dogerel" has spoilt the entertainment, almost sobbing with repressed anger, he then regains control and redirects proceedings with *Thop* 933-35.

It is his second redirection in as many Tales, for after the *Prioress's Tale* the pilgrims look so "sobre" that the Host lightens the mood by teasing Chaucer. Why such sobriety? Here Golden Clarioun creates a new oral possibility from the versatile text. Telling her Tale, the Prioress's voice bursts with affection at each image of childhood. Each mention of Jews, evil incarnate, fills her voice with righteous indignation in all its varieties. For example, at *PriT* 564 she shifts from Satan's voice back to her own voice, now gasping with rage. As she had prayed devoutly to Mary with *PriT* 467-80, so too she prays the last stanza. Her voice becomes louder, trembling at the horrid events she has related, events so like the recent ones in Lincoln brought on (sob) by sinful folk just like us (sob) so undeserving (sob) of God's mercy (waaah). Although no critic has proposed that the Prioress cries her last stanza, hysteria here does make good sense of the hush that follows. All the men in *Thop* 691-92 are sober not because of the story but because of discomfort while its teller is calmed down, patted presumably by the Second Nun and shielded from view by the Nun's Priest.

The Host takes control by calling on a very shy person, indeed fearful in *Thop* 707-9. In the ensuing narrative, at only two points does Chaucer-the-author chuckle outright (*Thop* 729, 744). Elsewhere, a naive reciter manages to recall not only all of the words, but also the minstrel inflections which he has laboriously memorized.

Partly because of very slow tempo, a performance feature which struggles magnificently against the implied quickness of the words on paper, a listener is ready to strangle the reciter by the sixth stanza. Yet on he goes, and on. And on. With adventure-show tones, Thopas heroically feeds his steed and flops down on the grass (*Thop* 778-83). With Jack-and-the-Beanstalk tones, the giant clomps onstage (*Thop* 807-16). With bright tones oblivious to the yawns around him, Chaucer-the-pilgrim bids lords to listen on (*Thop* 833-34). With fussy precision he assembles all details of food and of armour. Without a pause he announces "The Second Fit," blissfully unaware that "holde youre mouth" might be anything but formulaic (*Thop* 888-91). Unfortunately the subtitle, read aloud as usual, here detracts a bit from the Host's angry interruption at *Thop* 919. Feelings badly hurt, Chaucer-the-pilgrim sniffs lines 926-28, regains self-control by 940, and then introduces the *Tale of Melibeus* which, Chaucer-the-author knows at line 956, will bore everybody. The Golden Clarioun Chaucer-the-pilgrim sobs his last line 966, to the end a fully consistent character effectively conveying the voices within voices of this complex text.

GOLDEN CLARIOUN, 30NPT, cassette.
The Nun's Priest's Tale.
Reader Paul Piehler.
1986.
Side 1, *NPT* 2767-3330 (46 min.).
Side 2, *NPT* 3331-3462 (10 min.).
Cover: Contents.

Golden Clarioun presents a feminist interpretation of the *Nun's Priest's Tale*, in which Pertelote heroically endures the foibles of the intellectual snob who married her at age seven (nights). When they wake up on the perch, at *NPT* 2889-91, Pertelote calms her husband without a hint of exasperation. He becomes increasingly agitated as he reconstructs details of the dream. At first, Pertelote's melodramatic quavers make her reply seem overdone. Gradually, though, one realizes that from long experience she knows that her husband pays no attention to information from elsewhere than books. Therefore, she is using a voice appropriate to oral delivery of Launcelot de Lake (*NPT* 3212) or another romance, in an attempt to focus Chaunticleer's attention on the practical advice that will follow.

By his line 2971, it has become obvious that her husband has not heard a single word she said since 2940. Instead, he has been thinking up stories *he* knows from Cato and elsewhere, in order to prove yet again that he can read and she can't (*NPT* 3120-21). He lectures on and on, as usual. Pertelote as usual falls back asleep, until line 3157 when he nudges her wing. She listens yet again to his self-satisfied self-love, including a half-sung "confusio" (*NPT* 3164) and a recurrent tone of "Oh, aren't you lucky to have me?" particularly audible on lines 3166 and 3202.

Compared to the chickens, vulpine characterization is less compelling. The fox speaks as if addressing a passing stranger, excepting a flash of repressed glee at line 3307; he thus seems a bit too smart for the big stupid grin implied by his line 3414. Chaunticleer's personality remains consistent, however, for in the fox's jaws he behaves just as he did waking from the dream. With little gasps he starts out trying to speak calmly, but by *NPT* 3410 is surely scared.

The narrator of the Tale is scared in a different way. A meek squeaky-voiced man whose eager "oh" before "yis, sir" conveys his nervousness in *NPT* 2816, the Nun's Priest sounds even more timid while denying misogynistic sentiments with a nervous chuckle in line 3262 and a long pause after 3266 until, perhaps, the Prioress gives him the nod to continue. Elsewhere he does just what he is supposed to do: he tells a story with lots and lots of morals, including lines 3338-41 as well as the obvious ones, and delivers a sincere benediction to close. He probably blushes redder than Pertelote's face at the Host's lines 3447-60, which even in a tone of attempted neutrality spew pointless poor taste.

GOLDEN CLARIOUN, 40Ga(1), 40Ga(2), 40Ga(3), three cassettes available separately.
Sir Gawain and the Green Knight.
Readers Kerrigan Prescott, Paul Piehler, Judy Lowder Newton, Arnold Henderson, Larry Robbins, Gilbert Robinson, Eric Stirley, Louise Dunlap.
1965.
Edition: J. R. R. Tolkien and E. V. Gordon (Oxford, 1967 [sic]).
40Ga(1), Side 1, Introduction (21 min.).
Side 2, *SGGK* 1-59, 221-31, 250-565 (26 min.).

40Ga (2), Side 1, 691-762, 1046-1318 (24 min.).
Side 2, 1372-1401, 1468-1557, 1623-47, 1668-89,
1733-1869, 1922-78, 1998-2068 (31 min.).
40Ga(3), Side 1, 2069-2468, 2479-2530 (27 min.).
Side 2, Blank.
Cover: Contents.

GOLDEN CLARIOUN, 41P1, cassette.
The Pearl.
Reader Paul Piehler.
1972.
Edition: E. V. Gordon (Oxford, 1963).
Side 1, 1-600 (37 min.).
Side 2, 601-1212 (38 min.).
Cover: Contents.

GOLDEN CLARIOUN, 44SrO, cassette.
Sir Orfeo.
Reader Paul Piehler.
1980.
Edition: *Fourteenth Century Verse and Prose*, ed. Kenneth
   Sisam (Oxford, 1964).
Side 1, 1-604 (34 min.).
Side 2, Blank.
Cover: Contents.

GOLDEN CLARIOUN, 45Ly, cassette.
Middle English Lyrics.

Readers Paul Piehler, Maj-Britt Piehler, David Williams, Abbott Conway.
1972.
Editions: A sheet supplied with the tape tells the source of each poem read, in one of six listed anthologies of ME verse.
Side 1, Nou sprinkes the sprai, I have a yong suster, Of everykune tre, Al nist be the rose, O Lord so swett ser Iohn, At the northe ende of seluer whyte, Bytuene Mersh and Aueril, The smylng mouth, Is tell yw my mynd, Dronken, Wer there outher in this toun, Swarte smekyd smethes, Ffor the nyghthe-mare, The last tyme I the wel woke, This enther day I mete a clerke, Y louede a child of this cuntre, Foweles in the frith, My lefe ys faren in a lond, Alone walkyng, O mestres whye, I am olde, Fayre-wele my ioye, All that I may swynk, May no man slepe, John Ball's letter (27 min., 44 sec.).
Side 2, The Lade Dame Fortune, Al it is fantam that we mid fare, Quanne hic se on rode, What ys he this lordling, Nu lith the clei-clot, Heih is thi kinestol, Nou goth sonne vnder wod, Wit was his nakede brest, Ye that pasen be the weyye, Gold & all this werdis wyn, Crist and Sainte Marie, Sainte Marie Virgine, Sainte Marie Cristes bur, Worldes blis ne last no throwe (28:56).
Cover: Contents.

GOLDEN CLARIOUN, 46Pi, cassette.
Piers Plowman (C Text).
Reader Paul Piehler.
1972.
Edition: Elizabeth Salter and Derek Pearsall (Arnold, 1969).

Side 1, 1.1-98, 2.1-205 (30 min.).
Side 2, 21.1-272 (29 min.).
Cover: Contents.

GOLDEN CLARIOUN, 70No, cassette.
The Towneley Play of Noah.
Readers Paul Piehler, Kerrigan Prescott, Judy Lowder Newton, and members of the Gawain Players of Berkeley, California.
1962.
Edition: *Fourteenth Century Verse and Prose*, ed. Kenneth Sisam (Oxford, 1959).
Side 1, Introduction (10 min.).
Side 2, Entire play (31 min.).
Cover: Contents.

HARMONIA MUNDI, HM 1106, record. Availability not checked.
Medieval English Music Anonymes des XIVe et XVe siècles.
Performers Ashley Stafford, Paul Elliott, Rogers Covey-Crump, Leigh Nixon, Paul Hillier.
1983.
Director Paul Hillier.
Edition: John Stevens, ed., *Medieval Carols*, vol. 4 of *Musica Brittanica* (London: Stainer & Bell, 1952).
Side 1, Eight Latin songs.
Side 2, Three Latin songs; Alleluia /A newe work (3 min., 40 sec.), Ther is no rose (3:38), Marvel not Joseph (8:03).
Cover: Drinkers from B.L. Egerton ms. 3307.
Enclosure: Sixteen-page booklet with introduction in French, German, and English, and texts with translations into all three languages.

HYPERION, A66094, record. Availability not checked.
Troubadour Songs and Medieval Lyrics.
Performers Paul Hillier, Stephen Stubbs, Lena-Liis Kiesel.
1982.
Producers Tony Faulkner and Edward Perry, engineer Martin Compton.
Side 1 (76.41 155-01-1), Five Provençal songs.
Side 2 (76.41 155-01-2), Two Latin songs; Worldes blis (5 min., 33 sec.).
Cover: David playing the harp, from B.L. Royal ms. 2A XXII, fol. 14b.
Enclosure: Sheet with texts and translations, uncredited.

LINGUAPHONE, 78 r.p.m. record. Availability not checked.
Pronunciation of Middle English.
Reader H. C. Wyld.
Linguaphone Institute, "Made in England."
Side 1, *GP* 1-50, 68-72.
Side 2, *PriT* 635-83.
Cover: Contents.

Although no date is given, this 78 r.p.m. record probably represents the first commercial production of Chaucer aloud. If so, the industry began unpropitiously. Like a new student reading Shakespeare, the reader ends every line, enjambed or no, with a pitch drop and firm pause. Strong caesuras are introduced into many *PriT* lines. Some final *es* rhyme with ModE "day"—e.g., "smale foweles," "ferne," (*GP* 9, 14)—and sometimes other words replace Chaucer's—e.g., "in the Tabard," "his beere," "afterward" (*GP* 20, *PriT* 635, 666). All is blanketed by an inoffensive monotone.

LISTEN FOR PLEASURE, 7101, two cassettes.
Geoffrey Chaucer's The Canterbury Tales.
Prunella Scales and Martin Starkie, reading Modern English abridgements from Nevill Coghill's translation of *M1rT*, *RvT*, *NPT*, *PardT*, and *WBP*.
1982.
ISBN #0-88646-077-8.

Not in Middle English.

MEDIEVAL SOUNDS, M-1, cassette.
Geoffrey Chaucer: General Prologue, Pardoner's Prologue, Tale.
Reader Henry Grinberg.
1986.
Side 1, *GP* 1-746.
Side 2, *GP* 747-858, *PardT* 329-968.
Cover: Contents.

This *GP* recording has to recommend it careful pronunciation, several clever features, and overall artistic consistency that encompasses a discomfiting finale in which all the pilgrims, drawn into unity by the ever-agreeable narrator, turn as a body to make open mockery of the Host behind his back. The occasional slips into ModE vowels involve minor words, except for a ModE "soong" in *GP* 122 and an out-and-out American "glas" in 198, plus an odd but repeated pronunciation of ME "knew(e)" to rhyme with ModE "day."

Although the clever features might grate in a less skillful performance, here they help convey the narrator's genial compliance in turn with each pilgrim's personality and point of view. Before the last name in the long list of medical authorities known by the Physician, for example, in *GP* 434 the narrator emits a distinct "whew!" He sings the Friar's "In principio"; he pinches his nose to imitate the Prioress's singing, and again for the Pardoner's hair (*GP* 254, 123, 679).

The narrator condemns no one. Nor is he fooled by anyone—not even by the Knight who, he knows full well, is motivated less by "worthynesse" than by "sovereyn prys" (*GP* 50, 67). Each pilgrim thinks well of himself; and the narrator agrees soothingly with the Friar, agrees with the Reeve in tones of crotchety secretiveness, agrees with the Clerk that those who pay should be prayed for first. He most assuredly agrees that what the Wife of Bath did in youth is nobody's business but her own. He questions her stance only in the distinctness of his switch to the Parson's devout tones. Then gradually we come to realize that we are hearing a Parson as self-satisfied as anybody else, preaching a sermon concerning exemplary parsons who much resemble himself (*GP* 477 ff.). The narrator even avoids overt condemnation while imitating the Summoner's harsh snarl and his simple-minded machismo that relishes a child-scaring appearance (e.g., *GP* 646, 658, 673-74).

Certainly the Host is no less self-deluded than any of the pilgrims, pompously "boold" in *GP* 755 and merry on the several occurrences of that term. Money is foremost in his concerns, as conveyed by "ahem" before line 760 and by other inflections. Still it seems harsh for the narrator, representing the flock, to laugh outright at references to the "juggement" of their self-appointed "governour" (*GP* 818, 813). The Host is no dupe, however, when he cooly silences the Pardoner at the close of the second selection on this tape. Some critics suggest that the Pardoner, carried away by his own eloquence in *PardT* 919-45, sincerely tries to sell pardons to the pilgrims. This Pardoner, instead, gets carried away by his own teasing. After chuckling at the Christ's-pardon benediction, *PardT* 916-18, he starts kidding the other pilgrims and keeps on long after the joke has worn thin. The Host is glad for the chance to make everyone else comfortable by silencing the Pardoner. His heartiness tips to decisive irritation only on the last two lines, *PardT* 954-55, to make sure that he is understood by one so insensitive to others' responses.

The Pardoner's insensitivity appears elsewhere in this performance. In his Prologue he eagerly confides his tactics, unaware that some would consider them evil or unsportsmanlike. Within his Tale he does not distinguish the characters very sharply; the little boy in the tavern speaks with melodrama not unlike that of the old man. However, he does give distinct characters to the three riotours: one is evil, one very stupid (*PardT* 816-18, 822-23), and the youngest fresh-faced and eager until corrupted by the fiend at *PardT* 844.

MHS, 4485, record. Availability not checked.
A Tapestry of Music for The Black Prince and His Knights.
St. George's Canzona.
1970s?
Director John Sothcott.
L. of C. #81-750425.

Songs and dances from Latin and European vernacular traditions; Sumer is icumen in (1 min., 45 sec.), Bryd one brere (3:10), Gabriel fram evene king sent (4:11), St. Thomas honour we (3:37).
Cover: Stylized cartoon of king and trumpeters. Essay by Frank Grubb on Edward the Black Prince (1330-1376), with reference to concurrent music and literature.

NCTE, EMC-65-2963/4, record. Alternate stock number, 78863R.
Our Changing Language.
Readers Evelyn Gott Burack, Raven I. McDavid, Jr.
1975.
Producer EMC Corp., St. Paul, Minnesota.
Side 1, band 1, Introduction to History of the English Language.
    band 2, *Beowulf* 710-24.
    band 3, *NPT* 2821-46.
    band 4, *Julius Caesar* 3.1.254-75.
    band 5, Modern British English.
Side 2, Regional (U.S.) Dialect Samples by Locality.
Cover: Suggestions for classroom use; texts read on Side 1, with translations for OE and ME, none credited; discussion of the twelve dialect areas and methods used for Side 2.

    In this secondary-school-level prepared lesson on the history of English, the Middle English is totally mispronounced. The opening lines to the *Nun's Priest's Tale* are read with no apparent awareness of the words' meanings. Nearly every cognate, such as "was," is modern American English. The most striking repeated mispronunciation occurs as an American short *a* for every occurrence of ME *ee*. The cluster *eek* rhymes with ModE "back," for example.

NCTE, 45787, two-cassette set. No longer available as three-record set, RL20-8.
The Sounds of Chaucer's English.
Readers Daniel Knapp, Niel K. Snortum.
1967.
NCTE Committee on Publications.
Side 1, Introduction, Consonants, Vowels; *BD* 291-308, 1314-29, *PF* 85-91, 99-105, 561-74, 680-92.
Side 2, *Tr* 1.1-21; 3.50-84, 239-259; 5.1828-55.
Side 3, *GP* 1-18; *KnT* 1995-2023, 2764-79; *MlrT* 3698-3720; *RvT* 4034-45.
Side 4, *WBT* 857-81; *PardT* 711-33; *NPT* 3375-97; *Retraction* 1081-87a.
Enclosure: 52-page booklet, with very full materials to accompany the recording: Backgrounds on the History of English and Chaucer's English; Phonology; Table of Vowel Equivalents; Record Script and (further explanatory) Notes; and Selections (read). No credit given for edition. Multiple copies available of booklet, as stock number 45779R.

The idea is good, to produce a recording of ME exercises for use in language labs. The execution is abominable. What was once a three-record set is now available only on very poorly produced cassettes. Faint even on a component tape player at full volume, they would be inaudible, voices buried in static, on audiovisual equipment of the quality available at many educational institutions. Production aside, though, the performance would put any student to sleep.

The lesson begins with consonant and vowel sounds, each demonstrated by sample words and sentences and followed by silence during which the student is to repeat aloud. A reading through each passage of text, then, is followed by readings of segments of it likewise followed by silences. The ME pronunciation is correct throughout.

The potentially useful material and format are delivered in an unchanging drone of inflated religio-tragic melodrama. Even in Modern English—"Cut 1A"—the reader speaks from the depths of the grave. At a few points this dreary tone happens to coincide with a possible interpretation of the text. Someone not fearful or angry or awed about the horrors of war, but merely beaten into submission by the dreary repetitiveness of its atrocities, might describe Mars's altar in this tone (*KnT* 1995-2023). Someone who regarded the whole of *Troilus and Criseyde* as very sad, very serious, and very moralistic might end Book 5 in tones of unmitigated tragedy.

Advanced Chaucer students might find rewarding and amusing a discussion of why this tone is utterly inappropriate for most passages performed. For example, after the build-up of ending Book 2 with Troilus in bed in a kankedort, why is it inappropriate that Pandarus lead in Criseyde and, at *Tr* 3.61, administer extreme unction? Why should the chorus of birds not close *Parliament of Fowls* with a dirge? If beginning students are sent to learn ME from this recording, however, they may well never return to your classroom but rather go straight from the language lab to register for an Accounting course instead.

The accompanying pamphlet contains potentially excellent material: all the sample sounds and passages in full, with additional discussion of them, and introductory essays including useful lists of false cognates and "Obsolete or Difficult Forms" of ME words frequently encountered. NCTE should consider re-recording and re-producing the same format.

NCTE, P4PM-4852, record. No longer available in any
   form. Also apparently distributed in the past by EAV, as
   TE 9107.
Selections from Chaucer / On Reading Chaucer.
Reader Henry Morgan Ayres.
1965?
Side 1, band 1, Discussion of OE; selections from *Beowulf*
   including the sea voyage, Beowulf's introduction in
   court, the Unferth episode, Grendel's approach to
   Heorot, and order for tomb.
Side 1, band 2, Discussion of ME; *GP* 1-46, 58-72; *NPT*
   2821-46.
Side 2 (P4PM-4853), Shakespeare, Gettysburg Address.

In an introductory essay read aloud, two extremes are posited as to correctness of ME pronunciation. At one end, one simply pronounces final *e*s as needed for meter, and lives with the bad rhymes created by ModE vowels. At the other extreme, one attempts to reproduce the reconstructed sounds of a language never heard from a native speaker. After practicing the text as a succession of ME sounds, a reader should add the expression:

> The more [expression] you put in, the greater the chance of being wrong. But after you have practiced the text just as a succession of words . . . it is legitimate then to try to read it as well as you can. For while knowledge of this sort [i.e.,

correct vowels] is a good thing, it ought to be used as an aid to literary satisfaction, not as a substitute for it.

This is the only scholar to go on record admitting the possibility that he will utter less-than-perfect ME sounds—as indeed he does, though no oftener than do most recorded readers. He leaves out the *gh* in "droghte," and gives ModE cognates for "to" twice (*GP* 2, 13, 14). Despite the statement giving aesthetic preference to expression over correctness, though, he performs blandly if at all. The narrator regards the Knight and the *NPT* widow both as ideals, but his own personality is muffled. At *GP* 29, a slight shift in tone suggests that we pilgrims well deserve to be "esed atte beste."

NONESUCH, H 71315, record.
A Medieval Christmas.
Reader Nicholas Linfield.
1975.
Director Joel Cohen, performers The Boston Camerata.
L. of C. #75-750648.
Editions: J. W. Bright, ed., *The Gospel of John in West-Saxon* (Boston: Heath, 1904); Celia and Kenneth Sisam, eds., *The Oxford Book of Middle English Verse* (Oxford: Clarendon, 1970).
Side 1, Songs and chants in Hebrew, Latin, and European vernacular languages; John 1.1-14 from the Anglo-Saxon Gospel (59 sec.).
Side 2, Songs and chants in Latin and European vernacular languages; *PriT* 467-87 (1:25), Hand by hand we shule us take (0:36).
Cover: Nativity scene from Pierpont Morgan copy of *Spiegel van den Leven ons Heren.* Essay by Joel Cohen on

performance of medieval Christmas music. Credits for all editions.
Enclosure: Four-page booklet with all texts and English translations, with commentary on each. Although the reading-aloud follows Robinson's second edition, the text reproduced and credited is W. W. Skeat's *Complete Works of Geoffrey Chaucer*, 2d ed. (Oxford: Oxford UP, 1900).

In the brief Chaucerian passage, grouped with other pieces praising Mary, pronunciation slides toward ModE only at "to" in *PriT* 477. The male reader sounds a bit tentative about content—it is, after all, a woman's prayer to a woman—but takes control by using a tone of publicly proclaimed prayer.

OELSEN FILMS, 30/50, record. Availability not checked.
Medieval Theatre: The Mystery and Miracle Plays.
1960s?
Creator Rhoda W. Van Meter, narrator Bert Holland, editor James H. Butler.
Lecture coordinated with filmstrip of same title; no enactments.

PLANT LIFE, PLR 043, record. Availability not checked.
Miri It Is: English Medieval Music from the 13th and 14th Centuries.
Performers Philip Astle, Paul Williamson, Paul Hillier, and The Noyse of Musitians (i.e., Alan Wilson, Philip Thorby, Stephen Henderson).

1982.
Producers Paul Astle, Paul Williamson, Roger Limb.
Edition: E. J. Dobson and F. Ll. Harrison, *Medieval English Songs* (London: Faber & Faber, 1979).
Side 1, Four instrumental songs; Bryd one breere (3 min., 6 sec.), Lullay lullay (4:12), Miri it is (1:35).
Side 2, Three instrumental songs; Gabriel fram heven-king (2:20), Ar ne kuth ich sorghe non (6:48), Edi be thu (3:27), Fuweles in the frith (1:06).
Cover: Page with musicians from Luttrell Psalter; notes on each song and on instruments.
Enclosure: Sheet with ME texts and translations by E. J. Dobson, credited.

PLEIADES, P250, record in six-unit series. Availability not checked.
Historical Anthology of Music in Performance. Vol. 2: Late Medieval Music.
Performers Collegium Musicum of U of Chicago and same of Southern Illinois U.
1960s?
Conductors Howard M. Brown and Wesley K. Morgan.
L. of C. #R68-3612.
Edition: Archibald T. Davison and Willi Apel, eds., *Historical Anthology of Music*, 2 vols. (Cambridge: Harvard UP, 1946).
Songs and dances from Latin and European vernacular traditions; Sumer is icumen in.
Cover: Introduction stressing that the performance is exemplary rather than definitive. Translations of all songs, with reference to their texts published by Harvard UP.

RADIO ARTS, two-cassette set.
The O/Aural Tradition, Parts I and II. Part I: Beowulf and the Grendel Kind. Part II: Beowulf and the Dragon.
Reader Robert P. Creed.
1978.
Producer Charles Potter, narrator Earl Hammond, technical director David Rapkin, script consultant John M. Foley. Music composed and performed by Mary Remnant. Winner of the Corporation for Public Broadcasting Awards for Local Drama Production and Best Program of the Year in 1978.
Edition: Francis P. Magoun (Harvard).
Tape 1, side 1, Opening of poem, swimming match with Breca.
side 2, Fight with Grendel, fight with Grendel's mother.
Tape 1 also includes translations by Burton Raffel of these passages, and four breaks for commentary on the poem by John M. Foley, Bruce Rosenberg, Donald K. Fry, and Mary Remnant.
Tape 2, side 1, Flashbacks, beginning of the dragon story.
side 2, Fight with the dragon, Beowulf's funeral.
Tape 2 also includes translations by Burton Raffel of these passages, and three breaks for commentary on the poem by John M. Foley, Bruce Rosenberg, and Donald K. Fry.

RCA, LM 6015, record in ten-unit series. Availability not checked.
The History of Music in Sound. Vol. 2: Early Medieval Music up to 1300.
Performers Bodley Singers, Frederick Fuller.

1953.
Editor Dom Anselm Hughes, artistic supervisor Basil Lam.
Songs and dances from Latin and European vernacular traditions; Worldes blis ne last no throwe, Sumer is icumen in, Fuweles in the frith.
Enclosure: Seventy-page booklet. It contains reproduction of Reading Rota ms.; inserted leaf adapting booklet from record's previous state as twenty-sided 78 r.p.m. records; introduction; texts, notated scores, translations, and notes for all songs performed; bibliography.

RECORDING FOR THE BLIND.
Special Note: At least ten readings from Chaucer are available, not for sale but rather for loan. These special tapes cannot be used on commercial tape players. The catalogue of holdings costs $14 prepaid. For more information write, or call (609) 452-0606.

SCOTT FORESMAN, P4RP-6532, record. No longer available in any form.
From the Prologue to the Canterbury Tales by Geoffrey Chaucer.
Reader Robert Diamond.
1963.
Producer Gilbert Altschul, ModE reader Peter Ustinov.
W. W. Skeat, ed., *The Works of Geoffrey Chaucer* (Oxford: Clarendon, 1894?).
Side 1, Discussion of Chaucer and his times; *GP* passages from Theodore Morrison's translation.

Side 2, Discussion of Chaucer and his times; *GP* 23-24, 30-46, 61, 67-84, 89-94, 99-119, 127-31, 142-45, 151-60, 163-68, 191-200, 207-9, 221-24, 233-52, 269-75, 279-80, 283-90, 293-96, 299-303, 309-13, 317-18, 321-22, 325-34, 341-42, 349-50, 357-72, 379-94, 398-400, 411-14, 421-26, 439-42, 445-46, 453-60, 467-82, 491-96, 524-32, 536-48, 552-58, 562-77, 584-94, 603-4, 615-18, 621-35, 666-72, 675-78, 693-704, 715-18.

Enclosures: This record was part of a kit (#3174) which also included a filmstrip, 35 copies of its entire sound track, and a chart showing the Ellesmere ms. pilgrims and a map of the roads to Canterbury. Edition credited to W. W. Skeat and Clarendon, with no date.

The ragged *GP* excerpts on this record would be difficult to use other than with its filmstrip. The excerpter had a tendency toward bowdlerization, eliminating for example the Squire's hot loving and the Wife's "oother compaignye in youthe" (*GP* 97, 461).

Through the early portraits the narrator keeps sounding bratty, oddly enough. At *GP* 157, for example, he sounds ready to toss a mudball at the "ful fetys" cloak of the Prioress, and run. Another emotion conveyed is that of squeamishness: at "deed or bledde" mice, at "poraille" particularly lepers, at the Summoner's complexion (*GP* 145, 247, 624-35). This tone of disgust is aimed most directly at the Reeve, compared to whom the Summoner seems morally neutral—comic, almost, in his never-ending battle against acne. Amused that lying enables the Pardoner to pocket more money than does the local parson (*GP* 703-4), this narrator has little sympathy for secular money-making, for he disapproves of the Merchant's "wynnyng" or at any rate of his bragging about it (*GP* 275).

One listens in vain for a consistent moral viewpoint from this narrator, that is, or even for inconsistent morals from one imaginable character. Pronunciation is usually accurate, but with several slips to ModE cognates including "he" in *GP* 117, and "well" for "weel" in 367.

SPOKEN ARTS, SA 918, record. Also available as cassette, SAC 7004 or SAC 8004 (with *GP* and *PardT* excerpts from SA 919).
Beowulf.
Readers Norman Davis, Nevill Coghill.
1969.
Director Arthur Luce Klein.
L. of C. # R66-3250.
Side 1, band 1, Introduction to the poem, band 2, Pronunciation and meter.
Side 2, band 1, 1-25, band 2, 405-55, band 3, 710-70, band 4, 1251-1305, band 5, 2538-91, band 6, 3137-82.
Cover: Page from ms. Cotton Vitellius A.15. Summary of *Beowulf*. Biographies and photographs of Davis and Coghill.

SPOKEN ARTS, SA 919, record. Also available as cassette, SAC 7004 or SAC 8004 (with *Beowulf* excerpts from SA 918).
Geoffrey Chaucer. Selections from The Canterbury Tales.
Readers Nevill Coghill, Norman Davis.
1966.
Director Arthur Luce Klein.
L. of C. #R66-3253.

W. W. Skeat, ed., *The Poetical Works of Geoffrey Chaucer*
(London: Oxford UP, 1906).
Side 1, band 1, "Geoffrey Chaucer and His Context" by
Nevill Coghill (7 min., 57 sec.), band 2, "Chaucer's
Pronunciation" by Norman Davis (7:31).
Side 2, band 1, *GP* 1-78 read by Davis (4:16), band 2, *GP*
118-50 read by Coghill (2:51), band 3, *PardT* 739-894
read by Davis (9:32).
Cover: Brief introduction to Chaucer. Biographies and
photographs of Coghill and Davis. William Blake's
engraving "Chaucers Canterbury Pilgrims."
Enclosures: Two copies of a four-page booklet, with Davis's
essay on "Chaucer's Pronunciation" and the texts read.
W. W. Skeat and Oxford University Press are given
credit for the edition.

The discussions of Chaucer's life and social context and of ME pronunciation are not effective. Secondary-school pupils, for whom the material seems intended, might well become less rather than more interested in fourteenth-century England upon learning that Christianity then inspired a brand-new ideal of honor called chivalry in war, courtesy in peace, and romantic love in sex, that all arts abruptly burst into bloom like the coming of spring, and so on—with nary a mention of plague, labor unrest, overtaxation for a futile war, or the like. The essay on ME pronunciation, read aloud from the accompanying booklet, is suitable for the printed page. A listener has no time to think about the phonetic distinctions being made, much less practice them.

The *CT* passages are well chosen but not well performed. The two readers project a limited range of emotions—heartiness, eagerness, indignation, foreboding, evil, and a few others. Thus, for example, the narrator announces Madame Eglentyne's name (*GP* 121) with eager vocal inflections very similar to those with which the youngest riotour muses on sole ownership of the gold (*PardT* 840-43). Then the apothecary sells poison with such sinister glee that he too must be in on the murder plot (*PardT* 859-67).

Among errors in pronunciation, the most noticeable are instances of unstressed final -*es* with ModE long-*a* sound instead of a schwa, for the rhyme sets strondes/londes and youres/oures (*GP* 13-14, *PardT* 785-86). The recording lacks sufficient attention to differences between aural and visual understanding.

SPOKEN WORD, 1, four-record set. No longer available in any form.
The Canterbury Tales, by Geoffrey Chaucer.
Reader Nevill Coghill.
1949.
Produced by British Broadcasting Corporation. Sixteen readers of Coghill's ModE translation.
Side 1, *GP* 1-27.

This four-record set opens with justification for broadcasting a translation of Chaucer over BBC radio: Chaucer himself was a great translator who wrote for oral delivery. The first 27 lines of the *General Prologue* are read in a gently explanatory voice, in order to convey "the music of his language" but not particularly the sense of the text. "Felaweshipe" (*GP* 26) veers toward ModE pronunciation.

SPOKEN WORD, 99705-7, record. No longer available in any form.
The Creation and Fall / Abraham and Isaac.
Carleton Hobbs, Deryck Guyler, John Glen, Mary O'Farrell, Howard Marion-Crawford, and John Forrest, reading Modern English prepared for this broadcast.
1970.
Director John Barton. Producer Raymond Raikes, for the British Broadcasting Corporation (BBC).
Not in Middle English. Composite of excerpts from Norwich, Chester, York, Brome, Hegge, and Wakefield plays.

SPOKEN WORD, 99706-5, record. No longer available in any form.
Noah's Flood.
John Laurie, Mary O'Farrell, Godfrey Kenton, Anthony Jacobs, and Deryck Guyler, reading Modern English prepared for this broadcast.
1970.
Director John Barton. Producer Raymond Raikes, for the BBC.

Not in Middle English. Composite of excerpts from Wakefield, Chester, and Newcastle plays.

SPOKEN WORD, 99707-3, record. No longer available in any form.
The Nativity.

Deryck Guyler, Godfrey Kenton, June Tobin, Norman Shelley, Rupert Davies, Vivienne Chatterton, Charles Leno, John Glyn-Jones, and Geoffrey Matthews, reading Modern English prepared for this broadcast.
1970.
Director John Barton. Producer Raymond Raikes, for the BBC.

Not in Middle English. Composite of excerpts from York, Chester, Hegge, Coventry, and Wakefield plays (including Second Sheperds' Play).

SPOKEN WORD, 99708-1, record. No longer available in any form.
The Betrayal, Trial and Crucifixion.
James McKechnie, Deryck Guyler, Howard Marion-Crawford, Denis Goacher, June Tobin, Anthony Jacobs, and Carelton Hobbs, reading Modern English prepared for this broadcast.
1970.
Director John Barton. Producer Raymond Raikes, for the BBC.

Not in Middle English. Composite of excerpts from York and Wakefield plays.

SPOKEN WORD, 99709-X, record. No longer available in any form.
The Resurrection.

James McKechnie, Deryck Guyler, Howieson Culff, and
  Cyril Shaps, reading Modern English prepared for this
  broadcast.
1970.
Director John Barton. Producer Raymond Raikes, for the
  BBC.
Not in Middle English. Composite of excerpts from York
  and Chester plays.

SPOKEN WORD, 99710-3, record. No longer available in
  any form.
The Play of the Sacrament / Pride of Life.
Howard Marion-Crawford and Malcolm Hayes, reading
  Modern English prepared for this broadcast.
1970.
Director John Barton. Producer Raymond Raikes, for the
  BBC.
Not in Middle English. Excerpts from each play.

SPOKEN WORD, 99711-1, record. No longer available in
  any form.
*Mary Magdalene / Mind, Will and Understanding / The
  Castell of Perseverance.*
Mary Wimbush, Anthony Jacobs, Carleton Hobbs, John
  Glen, June Tobin, Trevor Martin, and Godfrey Kenton,
  reading Modern English prepared for this broadcast.
1970.
Director John Barton. Producer Raymond Raikes, for the
  BBC.

Not in Middle English. Excerpts from each play.

SPOKEN WORD, 99712-X, record. No longer available in any form.
Everyman. Readers Godfrey Kenton, Deryck Guyler, Ralph Truman, John Glen, Carleton Hobbs, Trevor Martin, and June Tobin. 1970. Director John Barton. Producer Raymond Raikes, for the BBC. Entire play in modernized pronunciation, with some deletions, modernizations, and interpolations.

APPENDIX:
RECORD COMPANY ADDRESSES

Music librarians bemoan the lack of any central listing system whatsoever for addresses of record companies. A search for such an address begins, most efficiently, on a physically existing album cover, and continues through such diverse sources as the Manhattan phone book; *The Folk Music Sourcebook*, ed. Larry Sandberg and Dick Weissman (New York: Knopf, 1976), 4-7; *Billboard International Buyer's Guide*, biannual from Billboard Publications, 9000 Sunset Blvd., Los Angeles, CA 90069; the NICEM index on microfiche, i.e., the *Index to Educational Records*, biennial from National Information Center for Educational Media, U of Southern California; *The Music Industry Directory*, 7th ed. (Chicago: Marquis, 1983), 589-610; and advertisements in a current Schwann's catalogue.

The process of providing addresses is further complicated by frequent merging, name-changing, and trading of labels by these foxlike record companies. Even the largest companies often take evasive action. Just during 1987, for example, Caedmon became an affiliate of Harper & Row Publishers, General Electric engulfed RCA Victor, Folkways moved from Manhattan to Princeton, and Argo changed its American distributor three times. Rather than attempt to trace all companies represented herein by one record apiece, in some cases I have not checked the currency of addresses printed on album covers. If line one of an item includes the note "Availability not checked," the address of its distributor has likewise not been checked.

ANZAMRS: The Chaucer Studio (ANZAMRS)
                   T. L. Burton
                   Dept. of English
                   University of Adelaide, GPO Box 498
                   Adelaide
                   South Australia 5001

ARGO: Argo Spoken Word
            Newman Communications Corp. 46 Wooburn
            2700 Broadbent Pkwy., N.E.   Manor Park
            Albuquerque, NM 87107   Wooburn Green
                                                 High Wycombe
                                                Bucks HP10 0ES
                                                England

BELLEROPHON: Bellerophon Books
                       36 Ana Capa St.
                       Santa Barbara, CA 93101

CAEDMON: Caedmon Records
                 Division of Harper & Row, Publishers
                 10 East 53rd St.
                 New York, NY 10022

CAMBRIDGE: Cambridge University Press
                    32 East 57th St.   200 Euston Rd.
                    New York, NY 10022   London NW1 2DB
                                           England

CAPITOL: Capitol Records / Angel Records
                    1370 Avenue of the Americas
                    New York, NY 10019

CASSETTE BOOK COMPANY: Cassette Book Company
                                      Box 7111
                                      Pasadena, CA 91109

COLUMBIA: Columbia Special Products
                    Division of CBS, Inc.
                    51 West 52nd St.
                    New York, NY 10019

DECCA: Decca Records
                    Division of MCA, Inc.
                    100 Universal Plaza
                    Universal City, CA 91608

DEUTSCHE GRAMMOPHON: Deutsche Grammophon
                                      /Polydor, Inc.
                                      1700 Broadway
                                       New York, NY 10019

EAV: Educational Audio Visual, Inc.
                  (formerly Lexington Records)   20 Peel St.
                  17 Marble Ave.   London, W8
                  Pleasantville, NY 10570   England

ENGLISH CLASSICS: No address found.

EVEREST: Everest Records
10920 Wilshire Blvd.
Los Angeles, CA 90024

EVERETT/EDWARDS: Everett/Edwards, Inc.
P. O. Box 1060
Deland, FL 32720

EXPERIENCES ANONYMES: Experiences Anonymes Recording Co.
141 Perry St.
New York, NY 10014

FOLKWAYS: Folkways/Scholastic Records
Birch Tree Group, Ltd.
180 Alexander St.
Princeton, NJ 08540

GOLDEN CLARIOUN: Golden Clarioun Literary Services
R. R. 1, Box 669
Hudson, Quebec, JOP 1H0
Canada

HARMONIA MUNDI: Harmonia Mundi, S.A.
04870 Saint-Michel de Provence
France

HYPERION: Hyperion Records, Ltd.
P. O. Box 25
London, SE9 1AX
England

LINGUAPHONE: No address found.

LISTEN FOR PLEASURE: Listen for Pleasure, Ltd.
          417 Center St.
          Lewiston, NY 14092

MEDIEVAL SOUNDS: Medieval Sounds
         P. O. Box 20400
         New York, NY 10025

MHS: Musical Heritage Society, Inc.
   14 Park Rd.   Enigma/Wealden Records
   Tinton Falls, NJ 07724 Old Forge Meadow
            Platts Heath
            Lenham, Maidstone, Kent
            England

NCTE: National Council of Teachers of English
       1111 Kenyon Rd.
       Urbana, IL 61801

NONESUCH: Elektra/Asylum/Nonesuch Records
       75 Rockefeller Plaza
       New York, NY 10019

OELSEN FILMS: No address found.

PLANT LIFE: Plant Life Records, Ltd.
       Edison Chambers
       107 Bancroft
       Hitchin, Hertfordshire
       England

PLEIADES: Pleiades Records
Harvard University Press
79 Garden St.
Cambridge, MA 02138

RADIO ARTS: Radio Arts
838 West End Ave., #6D
New York, NY 10025

RCA: Label sold by General Electric to a West German firm.

RECORDING FOR THE BLIND:
Recording for the Blind, Inc.
20 Roszel Rd.
Princeton, NJ 08540

SCOTT FORESMAN: Scott, Foresman & Co.
1900 East Lake Ave.
Glenview, IL 60025

SPOKEN ARTS: Spoken Arts
310 North Ave.
New Rochelle, NY 10801

SPOKEN WORD: Presumed defunct by a BBC representative.

INDEX
ARRANGED ACCORDING TO WORKS OF LITERATURE, IN THREE PARTS:

I. Chaucer Recordings, Arranged According to Abbreviated Titles of Works, with Readers or Performers

II. Recordings of Middle English Excluding Chaucer, Arranged According to Known Author or Common Title, with Readers or Performers

III. Recordings of Old English, Arranged According to Known Author or Common Title, with Readers

N.B.: Works available only translated into ModE are not indexed. Most references lead to excerpts, not to entire works.

I. INDEX TO CHAUCER RECORDINGS, ARRANGED ACCORDING TO ABBREVIATED TITLES OF WORKS, WITH READERS OR PERFORMERS

Adam= Chaucers Wordes unto Adam, His Owne Scriveyn.
    Caedmon TC 1226, by Jess B. Bessinger, Jr.   31

Argo PLP 1002, by John Burrow, Nevill Coghill, or
  Norman Davis 9
Astr= Treatise on the Astrolabe.
Cadmon SWC 3008, by Jess B. Bessinger, Jr. 33
BD= Book of the Duchess.
Golden Clarioun 2BD, by Paul Piehler 56
NCTE 45787, by Daniel Knapp or Niel K. Snortum 97
Bukton= Lenvoy de Chaucer a Bukton.
Argo PLP 1002, by John Burrow, Nevill Coghill, or
  Norman Davis 9
ClT= Clerk's Tale.
Golden Clarioun 19ClT, by Paul Piehler 78
FriT= Friar's Tale.
Golden Clarioun 17FrT, by Paul Piehler 75
FrkT= Franklin's Tale.
Golden Clarioun 22FkT, by Paul Piehler 81
GP= General Prologue to the Canterbury Tales.
Argo PLP 1001, by John Burrow, Nevill Coghill, or
  Norman Davis 7
Bellerophon, by Charles Muscatine 20
Caedmon TC 1151, by Jess B. Bessinger, Jr. 27
Caedmon SWC 3008, by Jess B. Bessinger, Jr. 33
Columbia AMS 6198, by Adele Addison 37
EAV LE 7650-55, by Helge Kökeritz 41
EAV KE 90233B, by Ronald A. Waldron 43
EAV KE 90395, by Helge Kökeritz 45
Golden Clarioun 10GP, by Paul Piehler and Maj-
  Britt Piehler 65
Golden Clarioun 10GPB, by Paul Piehler 66
Linguaphone, by H. C. Wyld 92
Medieval Sounds M-1, by Henry Grinberg 93
NCTE 45787, by Daniel Knapp or Niel K. Snortum 97
NCTE P4PM-4852, by Henry Morgan Ayres 99
Scott Foresman P4RP-6532, by Robert Diamond 104

Medieval English: A Discography

    Spoken Arts SA 919, by Nevill Coghill and Norman
        Davis   106
    Spoken Word 1, by Nevill Coghill   108
HF= House of Fame.
    Golden Clarioun 3HF(1) and 3HF(2), by Paul
        Piehler and Kerrigan Prescott   57
KnT= Knight's Tale.
    Argo ZPL 1208-10, by Richard Bebb and five other
        readers   14
    Golden Clarioun 11KnT, by Paul Piehler   68
    NCTE 45787, by Daniel Knapp or Niel K. Snortum   97
Lak= Lak of Stedfastnesse.
    Argo PLP 1002, by John Burrow, Nevill Coghill, or
        Norman Davis   9
    Caedmon TC 1226, by Jess B. Bessinger, Jr.   31
    Folkways FL 9859, by Victor L. Kaplan   53
MctT= Merchant's Tale.
    Cambridge, by A. C. Spearing   35
    Golden Clarioun 20MeT, by Paul Piehler   79
Merciles Beaute.
    Caedmon TC 1226, by Jess B. Bessinger, Jr.   31
M1rT= Miller's Tale.
    Caedmon SWC 1223, by Jess B. Bessinger, Jr.   29
    Golden Clarioun 12MiT, by Paul Piehler   70
    Cambridge, by A. C. Spearing?   35
    NCTE 45787, by Daniel Knapp or Niel K. Snortum   97
NPT= Nun's Priest's Tale.
    Argo PLP 1002, by John Burrow and three other
        readers   9
    Caedmon TC 1008, by Robert Ross   22
    EAV KE 90233B, by Ronald A. Waldron   43
    English Classics XTV 17216-17, by Kemp Malone   47
    Folkways FL 9859, by Victor L. Kaplan   53
    Golden Clarioun 30NPT, by Paul Piehler   87

NCTE EMC-65-2963/4, by unidentified reader 96
NCTE 45787, by Daniel Knapp or Niel K. Snortum 97
NCTE P4PM-4852, by Henry Morgan Ayres 99
PardT= Pardoner's Tale.
    Argo ZPL 1211, by Frank Duncan and three other readers 17
    Caedmon TC 1008, by Robert Ross 22
    Folkways FL 9859, by Victor L. Kaplan 53
    Golden Clarioun 24PdT, by Paul Piehler 82
    Medieval Sounds M-1, by Henry Grinberg 93
    NCTE 45787, by Daniel Knapp or Niel K. Snortum 97
    Spoken Arts SA 919, by Norman Davis 106
ParsP= Parson's Prologue.
    Caedmon TC 1151, by Jess B. Bessinger, Jr. 27
PF= Parliament of Fowls.
    ANZAMRS 1, by thirteen readers 3
    Caedmon TC 1226, by Jess B. Bessinger, Jr. 31
    Golden Clarioun 5PF, by Paul Piehler 59
    NCTE 45787, by Daniel Knapp or Niel K. Snortum 97
PLGW= Prologue to the Legend of Good Women.
    Argo PLP 1002, by John Burrow, Nevill Coghill, or Norman Davis 9
    Caedmon TC 1021, by Frank Silvera 23
PriT= Prioress's Tale.
    EAV KE 90395, by Helge Kökeritz 45
    Golden Clarioun 26PrT, by Paul Piehler 84
    Linguaphone, by H. C. Wyld 92
    Nonesuch H 71315, by Nicholas Linfield 100
Purse= Complaint of Chaucer to His Purse.
    Argo PLP 1002, by John Burrow, Nevill Coghill, or Norman Davis 9
    Caedmon TC 1226, by Jess B. Bessinger, Jr. 31
    Folkways FL 9859, by Victor L. Kaplan 53

Retraction= Retraction to the Canterbury Tales.
Caedmon TC 1151, by Jess B. Bessinger, Jr.   27
NCTE 45787, by Daniel Knapp or Niel K. Snortum   97
Rom= Romance of the Rose.
Golden Clarioun 1RR, by Paul Piehler   55
RvT= Reeve's Tale.
Caedmon SWC 1223, by Jess B. Bessinger, Jr.   29
Golden Clarioun 13ReT, by Paul Piehler   71
NCTE 45787, by Daniel Knapp or Niel K. Snortum   97
Scogan= Lenvoy de Chaucer a Scogan.
Caedmon TC 1226, by Jess B. Bessinger, Jr.   31
SumT= Summoner's Tale.
Golden Clarioun 18SuT, by Paul Piehler   76
Thop= Tale of Sir Thopas.
Golden Clarioun 27TST, by Paul Piehler   84
To Rosemounde.
Caedmon TC 1226, by Jess B. Bessinger, Jr.   31
Tr= Troilus and Criseyde.
Argo ZPL 1003-4, by Derek Brewer and four other readers   11
EAV LE 7650-55, by Helge Kökeritz   41
EAV KE 90395, by Helge Kökeritz   45
Golden Clarioun 6Tr(1) and 6Tr(2), by Paul Piehler and three other readers   61
NCTE 45787, by Daniel Knapp or Niel K. Snortum   97
Truth.
Argo PLP 1002, by John Burrow, Nevill Coghill, or Norman Davis   9
WBP= Wife of Bath's Prologue.
Argo SAY 23, by Prunella Scales and Richard Bebb   4
Cambridge, by Elizabeth Salter?   35
Columbia AMS 6198, by Adele Addison   37
EAV KE 0296, by Norman Davis   39
EAV KE 90395, by Helge Kökeritz   45

Golden Clarioun 16WBP, by Paul Piehler   72
WBT= Wife of Bath's Tale.
Argo SAY 23, by Prunella Scales and Richard Bebb   4
Cambridge, by Elizabeth Salter?   35
EAV KE 0296, by Norman Davis   39
Folkways SC 9851, by Charles W. Dunn   51
Golden Clarioun 16WBT, by Paul Piehler   73
NCTE 45787, by Daniel Knapp or Niel K. Snortum   97

II. INDEX TO RECORDINGS OF MIDDLE ENGLISH
EXCLUDING CHAUCER, ARRANGED ACCORDING
TO KNOWN AUTHOR OR COMMON TITLE,
WITH READERS OR PERFORMERS

Ancrene Riwle
   Caedmon SWC 3008, by Jess B. Bessinger, Jr.   33
Banns
   Caedmon SWC 1030, by Frank Silvera or others   25
William Caxton's Prologue to Eneydos
   Caedmon SWC 3008, by Jess B. Bessinger, Jr.   33
   EAV LE 7650-55, by Helge Kökeritz   41
Everyman
   Argo SAY 107, by Cyril Luckham, Gerald Harper,
     and Gary Watson   7
   Caedmon SWC 1031, by Burgess Meredith and
     others   25
   Spoken Word 99712-X, by seven BBC readers   112
James I's Kingis Quair
   Argo ZPL 1008, by Duncan McIntyre   13
John of Trevisa's Account of the Languages of Britain
   EAV LE 7650-55, by Helge Kökeritz   41

Layamon's Brut
   Caedmon SWC 3008, by Jess B. Bessinger, Jr.   33
Lyric poems/songs (*see also* Sumer is icumen in)
   Argo ZPL 1008, by four readers   13
   Caedmon SWC 3008, by Jess B. Bessinger, Jr.   33
   Decca DL 9418, by New York Pro Musica   38
   Everest 3145/7, by New York Pro Musica   49
   Experiences Anonymes 0024, by three singers   50
   Experiences Anonymes 0029, by Russell Oberlin   50
   Golden Clarioun 45Ly, by Paul Piehler and three other readers   89
   Harmonia Mundi HM 1106, by Paul Hillier and four other singers   91
   Hyperion A66094, by Paul Hillier and two other singers   92
   Nonesuch H 71315, by Nicholas Linfield   100
   Plant Life PLR 043, by Paul Hillier and five other singers   101
Thomas Malory's Book of King Arthur
   Caedmon SWC 1054, by Cambridge University members   26
   Caedmon SWC 1374, by Siobhan McKenna   33
   Caedmon SWC 3008, by Jess B. Bessinger, Jr.   33
Robert Mannyng's Story of Englande
   Caedmon SWC 3008, by Jess B. Bessinger, Jr.   33
Dan Michel's Ayenbite of Inwyt
   Caedmon SWC 3008, by Jess B. Bessinger, Jr.   33
A Moral Tale in Fourteenth-Century Kentish
   EAV LE 7650-55, by Helge Kökeritz   41
Noah (Wakefield/Towneley play)
   Golden Clarioun 70No, by Paul Piehler and others   91
Pearl
   Caedmon TC 1192, by Jess B. Bessinger, Jr. and Marie Borroff   29

Golden Clarioun 41Pl, by Paul Piehler 89
Piers Plowman
   Argo SAY 107 (ModE) 7
   EAV LE 7650-55, by Helge Kökeritz 41
   Golden Clarioun 46Pi, by Paul Piehler 90
Richard Rolle's Bee and the Stork
   Caedmon SWC 3008, by Jesse B. Bessinger, Jr. 33
Sir Gawain and the Green Knight (*SGGK*)
   Caedmon TC 1192, by Jess B. Bessinger, Jr. and
     Marie Borroff 29
   Caedmon SWC 3008, by Jess B. Bessinger, Jr. 33
   EAV LE 7650-55, by Helge Kökeritz 41
   Folkways SC 9851, by Charles W. Dunn 51
   Golden Clarioun 40Ga(1), 40Ga(2), and 40Ga(3),
     by Paul Piehler and seven other readers 88
Sir Orfeo
   Golden Clarioun 44SrO, by Paul Piehler 89
Sumer is icumen in (*see also* Lyric poems/songs)
   Argo (Z)RG (5)443, by twelve singers 20
   EAV LE 7650-55, by Helge Kökeritz 41
   MHS 4485, by St. George's Canzona 95
   Pleiades P250, by Collegium Musicum groups 102
   RCA LM 6015, by Bodley Singers 103
Wyclif-Purvey translation of the Bible
   EAV LE 7650-55, by Helge Kökeritz 41

III. INDEX TO RECORDINGS OF OLD ENGLISH,
ARRANGED ACCORDING TO KNOWN AUTHOR OR
COMMON TITLE, WITH READERS

Aelfric's Homily
   Caedmon SWC 3008, by Jess B. Bessinger, Jr. 33

Medieval English: A Discography

EAV LE 7650-55, by Helge Kökeritz	41
Alfred's Preface to Pope Gregory's Pastoral Care	
Caedmon SWC 3008, by Jess B. Bessinger, Jr.	33
Anglo-Saxon Chronicles (*see also* Battle of B./M.)	
Caedmon SWC 3008, by Jess B. Bessinger, Jr.	33
Anglo-Saxon Gospel	
EAV LE 7650-55, by Helge Kökeritz	41
Nonesuch H 71315, by Nicholas Linfield	100
Battle of Brunanburh	
Caedmon SWC 1161, by Jess B. Bessinger, Jr.	28
Battle of Maldon	
Argo SAY 73 (ModE)	6
Caedmon SWC 1424, by Kemp Malone	33
Caedmon SWC 3008, by Jess B. Bessinger, Jr.	33
Folkways SC 9851, by Charles W. Dunn	51
Bede's Death Song	
Folkways FL 9858, by Robert P. Creed	52
Beowulf	
Argo SAY 73 (ModE)	6
Caedmon SWC 1161, by Jess B. Bessinger, Jr.	28
Caedmon SWC 3008, by Jess B. Bessinger, Jr.	33
Caedmon TC 4001, by Kemp Malone	35
EAV KE 90395, by John C. Pope	45
EAV LE 7650-55 by Helge Kökeritz	41
Folkways SC 9851, by Charles W. Dunn	51
NCTE EMC-65-2963/4, by unidentified reader	96
NCTE P4PM-4852, by Henry Morgan Ayres	99
Radio Arts, by Robert P. Creed	103
Spoken Arts SA 918, by Nevill Coghill and Norman Davis	106
Caedmon's Hymn	
Caedmon SWC 1161, by Jess B. Bessinger, Jr.	28
Caedmon SWC 3008, by Jess B. Bessinger, Jr.	33
Folkways SC 9851, by Charles W. Dunn	51

  Folkways FL 9858, by Robert P. Creed   52
Charm fragment
  Folkways FL 9858, by Robert P. Creed   52
Dream of the Rood
  Caedmon SWC 1161, by Jess B. Bessinger, Jr.   28
  Caedmon SWC 1424, by Kemp Malone   33
Earth Mother of Men
  Caedmon SWC 1424, by Kemp Malone   33
Genesis
  Caedmon SWC 1424, by Kemp Malone   33
  Folkways FL 9858, by Robert P. Creed   52
Husband's Message
  Folkways FL 9858, by Robert P. Creed   52
Riddles
  Folkways FL 9858, by Robert P. Creed   52
Ruin
  Folkways FL 9858, by Robert P. Creed   52
Seafarer
  Folkways SC 9851, by Charles W. Dunn   51
Wanderer
  Caedmon SWC 1161, by Jess B. Bessinger, Jr.   28
  Caedmon SWC 1424, by Kemp Malone   33
Wife's Lament
  Caedmon SWC 1161, by Jess B. Bessinger, Jr.   28
  Caedmon SWC 1424, by Kemp Malone   33
Wulf and Eadwacer
  Caedmon SWC 1424, by Kemp Malone   33
  Folkways FL 9858, by Robert P. Creed   52
Wulfstan's Sermo ad Anglos
  Caedmon SWC 3008, by Jess B. Bessinger, Jr.   33